Decolonial Imaginaries in Palestinian Experimental Film and Video

Decolonial Imaginaries in Palestinian Experimental Film and Video focuses on an underexamined group of female Palestinian filmmakers, highlighting their relevance for thinking through a diverse set of issues relating to decolonial aesthetics, post-nationalism and gender, non-Western ecologies, trauma and memory, diasporic experiences of space, biopolitics, feminist historiography and decolonial temporalities.

Positing that these filmmaker-artists radically counter dominant media images of Palestinians, deessentializing Palestinian identity while opening up history and the present to new potentialities and ways of imagining Palestinian futures, *Decolonial Imaginaries in Palestinian Experimental Film and Video* argues that Palestinian experience is urgently relevant to all of us. As the works address issues of food availability and land use, environmental collapse and forced displacement, Hole explores how such films generate hope, imagine impossible possibilities and offer inspiration and wisdom when it comes to losing and rebuilding.

Addressing a fundamentally transnational and understudied area, this book will resonate with readers working in the areas of film and media studies, Palestinian cultural studies, historiography, Middle East studies and experimental film.

Kristin Lené Hole is Associate Professor of Film Studies in the School of Film at Portland State University, USA. She is the author of *Towards a Feminist Cinematic Ethics: Claire Denis, Emmanuel Levinas, and Jean-Luc Nancy*.

Routledge Focus on Film Studies

Virtue and Vice in Popular Film
Joseph H. Kupfer

Unproduction Studies and the American Film Industry
James Fenwick

Indian Indies
A Guide to New Independent Indian Cinema
Ashvin Immanuel Devasundaram

Migration and Identity in British East and Southeast Asian Cinema
Leung Wing-Fai

Con Artists in Cinema
Self-Knowledge, Female Power, and Love
Joseph H. Kupfer

The Body in Jean-Luc Godard's New Wave Films
Francesca Minnie Hardy

Jürgen Böttcher and Documentary Film
Documentaries, Contemporaries, History
Elizabeth Daggett Matar

Decolonial Imaginaries in Palestinian Experimental Film and Video
Postnational and Feminist Aesthetics
Kristin Lené Hole

For more information about this series, please visit: www.routledge.com/Routledge-Focus-on-Film-Studies/book-series/RFFS

Decolonial Imaginaries in Palestinian Experimental Film and Video

Postnational and Feminist Aesthetics

Kristin Lené Hole

LONDON AND NEW YORK

First published 2024
by Routledge
4 Park Square, Milton Park, Abingdon, Oxon OX14 4RN

and by Routledge
605 Third Avenue, New York, NY 10158

Routledge is an imprint of the Taylor & Francis Group, an informa business

British Library Cataloguing-in-Publication Data
A catalogue record for this book is available from the British Library

Library of Congress Cataloging-in-Publication Data
Names: Hole, Kristin Lené, author.
Title: Decolonial imaginaries in Palestinian experimental film and video : postnational and feminist aesthetics / by Kristin Lené Hole.
Description: London ; New York : Routledge, 2024. | Series: Routledge focus on film studies | Includes bibliographical references and index.
Identifiers: LCCN 2024008144 (print) | LCCN 2024008145 (ebook) | ISBN 9781032755397 (hardback) | ISBN 9781032755403 (paperback) | ISBN 9781003474449 (ebook)
Subjects: LCSH: Motion pictures—Palestine. | Experimental film—Palestine. | Women in the motion picture industry—Palestine. | Palestine—In motion pictures.
Classification: LCC PN1993.5.P35 H65 2024 (print) | LCC PN1993.5.P35 (ebook) | DDC 791.43095694—dc23/eng/20240222
LC record available at https://lccn.loc.gov/2024008144
LC ebook record available at https://lccn.loc.gov/2024008145

ISBN: 978-1-032-75539-7 (hbk)
ISBN: 978-1-032-75540-3 (pbk)
ISBN: 978-1-003-47444-9 (ebk)

DOI: 10.4324/9781003474449

Typeset in Times New Roman
by Apex CoVantage, LLC

Contents

Figures

Acknowledgments

I'd like to thank Dr. Mark Berrettini for being the first set of eyes on most of these chapters. A version of the last chapter was published in the *Middle East Journal of Culture and Communication*, and I'd like to thank my two reviewers and my reviewer at Routledge for their comments on and support for the work. Courtney Hermann generously delayed her own sabbatical to chair our program, which enabled me to take my sabbatical and write this book. Brian Berry looked over a draft of my introduction. My daughter, Pola Cowan, asked me a lot of questions about Palestine and took an interest in what I was writing that meant a lot to me. She is part of a generation who will grow up with a very different picture of Israel than previous generations in this country. I was fortunate to participate in the daily WAWOG writing group meetings in December of 2023, which gave me structure and encouragement and lessened the isolation I felt as I finished the introduction. My thoughts throughout the editing process have been with all Palestinians, especially those in Gaza right now, suffering genocide and mass displacement. This book is for them and dedicated to their freedom.

Preface: Writing in a Time of Genocide

I wrote the bulk of this book over the course of a sabbatical during the academic year 2022–23 and submitted it to the publisher in the summer of 2023. Of course, at that time, I had no idea what would unfold in the fall of 2023—Israel's explicit and accelerated attempt to destroy Gaza and to kill or displace all Palestinians in Gaza under the pretext of eradicating Hamas and rescuing Israeli hostages. I will not unpack the competing discourses that have dominated the media landscape all season, the discursive struggle that Israel largely controls and the inability of so many in the West to mourn Arab, Palestinian lives. My research over the past years on Palestine makes me aware that while this is a particularly devastating moment in Palestinian history, it is nothing new. In some ways it makes visible the reality of the occupation and the violence and abuse that Palestinians are subject to on a daily basis, in a way that makes it much harder for the world to overlook. At moments, I do feel the tide of public awareness and opinion shifting where I am writing, in the United States, Israel's best friend and unwavering ally.

The events of this fall have altered something at a deeper level in me. I had in many ways become complacent. I've ascended the class I was born into, and I have a salaried university position. I get to have a career where I can write and teach about systemic oppression and global inequality and hope I have an impact on how people think about the world. But I'm more or less comfortable with the status quo and appreciate that it is there for me to be critical of intellectually. This fall, something from a younger time in my life is loosening and floating to the surface of my sense of self and world: the profound and clear belief that our world needs to change in ways that will make it unrecognizable to us now. We need more than a ceasefire. Palestine needs so much more than a ceasefire. I have learned this from the films I write about in this book and the paths of study down which they have led me.

I am not an expert on these films but a student of them. They have taught me not just about Palestine but about what it means to be a settler colonist where I live, how the environment is deeply connected to who we are and where we are and how relations of domination and power mark and destroy the world in which we live and the food that we eat. They have challenged modernist nationalisms and taught me of the generative futurisms that can emerge when hope seems completely lost, but the imagination is strong and beautiful. Through these films, I came to know Palestine as a land of strong and resilient people, women especially. I began to see it as a source of wisdom about what it means to rebuild the world, over and over. I saw Palestine as the source of formally and conceptually challenging art that made me think about visuality and history in much more nuanced ways. Palestine as a place of diverse music traditions, Palestine as a way to rethink time and space, Palestine as a microcosm through which we can think about identity, memory and inheritance. Palestine in these films is not suffering speechless victims. It is not the Palestine that media coverage has reinforced over the past several months (when it has not conflated Palestine with terrorism). Throughout this war on Gaza, I have held on to the Palestine I know through these films, and despite the devastation and the grief, I have retained their radical visions. Likewise, writers with a long and reflective gaze, like Edward Said and Raja Shehadeh, have given me solace in a culture where information comes fast and furious and the mind and body react chaotically to the surge of data. In reflecting on his own anger at Israel's success in eroding the territory of the West Bank, making his wanderings through the hills increasingly impossible, Raja Shehadeh notes that "More than anything else it was writing that was helping me overcome the anger that burns in the heart of most Palestinians."[1] When Shehadeh looks at the "monumental crusader castles in a dilapidated state" that "dot the land," he realizes regarding the Israeli settlements and roads that cut up the landscape that "the stronger the attempt at impressing me with their permanence, the more my mind sought confirmation of their transience."[2]

I have only made minor changes to the book despite Israel's massacre of Gazans this fall and winter. I am deeply uncomfortable writing about things as they are happening, especially in such a permanent form as an academic book, and I also feel highly ambivalent about the possibility that my work will suddenly have more currency because of the suffering and mass murder of Gazans. Stating that, I am committed to the visions of Palestine in these films and believe that the countermemories and images they so generously offer are perhaps more necessary than ever. This is a transient moment, and as I grieve and denounce what is happening, Palestinian filmmaking and writing offer a space of reflection and regeneration that reinforce my belief that if the present is Zionist, the future is Palestinian, where Palestinian signifies a way forward based on ecology, plurality, decoloniality and beauty.

Notes

1 Raja Shehadeh, *Palestinian Walks: Notes on a Vanishing Landscape* (London: Profile Books, 2007), 171.
2 Shehadeh, *Palestinian Walks*, 170.

Bibliography

Shehadeh, Raja. *Palestinian Walks: Notes on a Vanishing Landscape*. London: Profile Books, 2007.

1 Introduction

Decolonial Imaginaries in Palestinian Experimental Film and Video: Postnational and Feminist Aesthetics

A woman stands in front of a film being projected, marking over its images with black streaks (Figure 1.1). The projected film is *Our Small Houses* (Kassem Hawal, 1974), filmed in the Palestinian refugee camp An-Nahar Al-Bared in northern Lebanon. Its images are grainy, blown up and often hard to discern. The woman who interrupts this film with her physical presence and actions is filmmaker-artist Basma Alsharif. In Alsharif's film, *O, Persecuted* (2014), she layers a distorted soundtrack of helicopters, machine guns and marching over these actions. In a calmer moment of acoustic and visual clarity, *O, Persecuted* highlights a sequence from the earlier film that emphasizes the necessity of killing or being killed. Eventually, footage of Boubouka, the Greek belly dancer, is superimposed over *Our Small Houses*, and *O, Persecuted* transitions from the militant film of the past to contemporary images of Israeli pool parties and raves. Happy drinkers, tight, bikini-clad bodies and images of decadence are cut to aggressive techno music, while a palimpsest of Boubouka's gyrating body lingers onscreen. The juxtaposition of the dispossessed Palestinians with the luxury and excess of the Israeli occupants suggests the failure of the project of Palestinian liberation. *O, Persecuted* explicitly references revolutionary Palestinian history and ironizes Israeli discourses of persecution while refusing to romanticize the past. Crucially, questions of national identity are intertwined with those of gender and sexuality through Boubouka's body and through the insertion of Alsharif herself, a diasporic Palestinian. *Our Small Houses*' documentation of dispossession and resistance is projected onto the filmmaker's body as she physically works over its historical narrative. *O, Persecuted* challenges the efficacy of images of Palestinian suffering as well as revolutionary modes of storytelling, given the worsening of Palestinian living conditions in the occupied territories over time.

Alsharif (b. 1983) is a filmmaker and multimedia artist whose work is often presented in installation contexts within gallery or museum spaces. She was born to Palestinian parents in Kuwait and raised in the United States, France and Gaza. Currently residing in Berlin, her adult life has continued to follow an itinerant global path. With this biography, Alsharif is what Laura U.

DOI: 10.4324/9781003474449-1

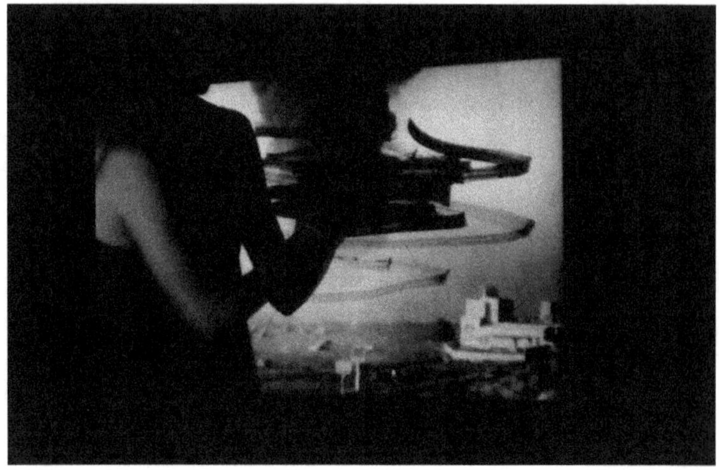

Figure 1.1 Alsharif marks over the 1974 film *Our Small Houses* in *O, Persecuted* (2014).

Marks (2002) would call an intercultural artist, or Hamid Naficy (2001) an "accented" filmmaker.[1] In *O, Persecuted*, her physical engagement with the earlier revolutionary film calls to mind the haptic dimensions of intercultural experimental films and the tactile optics of accented cinema.[2] The footage of Alsharif marking over the earlier film is shown in reverse, as if she could undo the past through her re-working, intervening in the temporal progression of events and in dominant representations of Palestine.

Although I turn to several other filmmakers throughout this book, my focus is on the films of three contemporary female Palestinian artists: Alsharif, Jumana Manna (b. 1988) and Larissa Sansour (b.1973). Like Alsharif, Manna and Sansour have biographies reflective of their nomadic status as Palestinians—Manna was born in the United States, raised in Palestine, studied in Norway and currently lives in Germany, whereas Sansour was born in East Jerusalem and has lived in the United States, England and Denmark, which she represented at the Venice Biennale in 2019. Alsharif, Manna and Sansour are all visual artists, where film or video work is one facet of larger art practices that include sculpture and installation. In this sense, they all straddle the film and fine art worlds. Sansour's work is rooted in speculative dystopian fiction. Her production values are high, with sets and costumes creating immersive worlds; her multi-channel pieces are particularly well-suited to museum and gallery exhibitions. Earlier in her career, Manna produced shorter experimental pieces, but her more recent films are documentaries engaging with questions of history, identity and land use. Alsharif has worked primarily in analog film formats, and her work is the most formally experimental of the three. These filmmakers are indicative of trends in experimental, often diasporic, work that explores issues of Palestinian identity, history, visuality, space and time in non-masculinist and post-nationalist modes.

Experimental Film

Not enough scholarly attention has been paid to experimental filmmaking from Palestine.[3] I've been struck by the fact that experimental filmmaking gets little discussion in the major books on Palestinian film, given that the conditions of exile, the fragmented relationship to home, the traumatic experience of time and the discursive gaslighting in the dominant media around Palestinian reality render experimental modes particularly suited to their representation. While writing, I have often thought about Fanon's description of the "zone of occult instability where the people dwell" and how experimental approaches seem most apposite for wrestling with the complexity of living in that zone of occult instability.[4] Furthermore, experimental work can, but does not always, require less of an institutional support structure than other forms of filmmaking: this is not the case per se with the films I discuss here, but it applies to some, and it makes sense that as a more accessible mode of audiovisual expression, experimental forms would hold a special place in Palestinian film. In Chapter 5, I note that in his book, *Surviving Images: Cinema, War, and Cultural Memory in the Middle East*, Kamran Rastegar argues that because of the unresolved nature of Palestinian statehood and the ongoing *Nakba*, Palestinianness is a fundamentally aporetic experience. While his book looks at narrative art cinema, rather than more experimental modes, he argues that "what remains most evocative of the Palestinian story is its frequent irreconcilability to traditional narrative forms."[5] In Chapter 5, I expand on his insight to talk about aporias of space, time and visuality in relation to Alsharif's work, but here I want to reiterate that practices of filmmaking that are not as rooted in editing patterns emphasizing the continuity of time and space, are less committed to making narrative sense and achieving closure, or that push our way of seeing and hearing to new places and ask us to reframe and rethink because of the very form they employ seem particularly suited to addressing an aporetic experience of the real.

In *After the Last Sky*, Edward Said notes that "no clear and simple narrative is adequate to the complexity of our experience" and that "wherever we are, we are dogged by our past, but we have also created new realities and relationships that neither fit simple categories nor conform to previously encountered forms."[6] Inevitably, Said is more articulate and authoritative here than I can be; his experience as a Palestinian and literary scholar brings him to the conclusion that Palestinianness requires new forms of expression, representation and narration. *After the Last Sky* is itself an experiment of sorts, with photos by the British photographer Jean Mohr elucidated by Said's keen observations and the ruminations they inspire on aspects of Palestinian life. He goes on to say that given that "Palestinian life is scattered, discontinuous, marked by the artificial and imposed arrangements of interrupted or confined space, by the dislocations and unsynchronized rhythms of disturbed time," he believes "that essentially unconventional, hybrid, and fragmentary forms of expression should represent us."[7]

In his book on *The Palestinian Idea*, Greg Burris advocates for Palestinian film as potentially revolutionary media, although again, I am struck by the fact that most of his examples are fairly conventional narratives. He argues that cinema is a site where Palestinian "plasticity" is rendered visible. What Burris means by plasticity derives from philosopher Catherine Malabou: plasticity ranges from the giving of form to the receiving of form to form's very annihilation. It is this third sense, plasticity as an exploding or annihilation of form, that Burris connects to what he calls, after Said, "the Palestinian idea." For Said, the Palestinian idea is not grounded in an ethnonationalist framework but in plurality, coexistence and equality. In Burris' adaptation of the concept, "equality is already being *enacted* and *mediated* in Palestine, and it is this scandalous affirmation—this assertion of equality amidst inequality—that I call 'the Palestinian idea.'"[8] The Palestinian idea is a political (in Rancière's sense of the political as an event that disrupts inequalities) challenge to identitarian forms that reproduce disparities and oppression. This deessentialization of identity will remain a theme throughout my analysis: the insistence on a fixed and closed definition for any group is inherently exclusionary and repressive in this framework. Plasticity destroys these constructed certainties; through its annihilation of form and its stance of refusal, it "clear[s] a path for the introduction of new possibilities."[9] Burris argues that Palestinian identity is open and negotiated in Palestinian cultural production; "at its best, film is also one of the places where the terms of Palestinian identity can be annihilated and new emancipatory policies can be brought into being."[10] This annihilation and open negotiation are driving forces in the films that comprise this book.

My readings of these films are in line with Burris' argumentation, particularly in his rejection of essentialist notions of identity and his assertion that "Nakba, dispossession, and death are not Palestine's only stories. Liberation is also a lived reality, and I believe that it can serve as a much more radical starting point for analysis than Zionism's victories."[11] Where I would push his analysis further, however, is his reliance on more conventional narrative cinema for his case studies through which to explore the Palestinian idea. While he argues that because of their situation "Palestinian filmmakers have a chance to create a new kind of cinema," the focus on content over form misses some of the radical potential of the argument he has so deftly expounded.[12] For, what explodes form more than experimentation with form, with narrative structure, with the dominant representational modes, which are themselves ideologically burdened with the weight of conventions established in the heart of empire? In Sansour's work with multiple channel installation and short-form open-ended storytelling, or in Alsharif's exploration of militarized modes of seeing and reversed footage, there is real potential to annihilate form and revise dominant representational economies, particularly as they position the Palestinian (if not as terrorist) as suffering victim, poor and ignorant, without imagination, joy or critical faculty. To return to Said, "Many of us have been killed, many permanently scarred and silenced, without a trace. And the images used to represent us only diminish our reality further."[13] This intervention into the larger representational landscape of Palestine is a significant facet of these films: Manna's revisionist historiographies that talk to ghosts of the Palestinian past to reimagine the present and her decolonial framings of Palestinian relationships in a full and fertile landscape are refusals of dominant representational tropes as well as invitations to Palestinian becoming (to borrow language from Gil Hochberg). Sansour's repositioning of the Palestinian woman as a guerilla archaeologist and "narrative terrorist" or as a radical botanist preserving biodiversity in an underground bunker after an ecological collapse, similarly opens Palestinianness up to plasticized reimaginings. Finally, Alsharif re-situates Gaza in a world historical map that is fluid and connected, a decolonial revisioning of time and space that refuses to represent the overrepresented Palestinian directly and instead follows Palestine's resonances across space and time. These filmmakers reject a well-known set of stereotypes, historical narratives and an overdetermined image repertoire to ask questions about Palestine and Palestinianness, to imagine other ways of being and to move out of a state of exceptionalism to seek connection across borders and histories.

I consider these works feminist, in that they offer non-ethnonationalist conceptions of Palestine (Manna's *A Magical Substance Flows into Me*, 2017); center women in their storytelling (Manna's documentaries and Sansour's films generally); offer decolonial perspectives on the land (Sansour's *In Vitro*, 2019, and Manna's *Wild Relatives*, 2018, and *Foragers*, 2022); and connect Palestinian experience with other global struggles against colonialism and racism (Alsharif's *Ouroboros*, 2017, and Manna's *Wild Relatives*). Alsharif's *O, Persecuted* is an example of how the gendered body can be used in formal experimentation to question failed nationalist paradigms. While the work of these artists may not always align with a narrow Western notion of what feminist representation looks like, these are Palestinian decolonial feminist statements.

What also interests me about their bodies of work is their exploration of Palestine and a Palestinian identity that are not rooted in revolutionary paradigms, which often rely on the nostalgic romanticization of a patriarchal, heteronormative and ethnically homogenous fantasy of the nation-state.[14] Alongside this is an insistence on a deessentialized plural notion of Palestinianness. Historically, the Zionist sense of entitlement to Palestinian land has been partly rationalized by claims that Palestinians do not really exist, be it literally (the land was 'empty') or as a historical and unified people group that differs from the Arab states that it neighbors. As Palestine faces the active threat of extermination, it feels particularly sensitive to claim an identity that is fluid and open to contestation from within—that is, a deessentialized Palestinianness. Yet, guided by these films, this book will insist on the openness of Palestinian identity to alternate imaginings, to inclusive interpellations and to a future to be determined by Palestinians themselves in all of their diversity. This is part of the truly radical nature of this work: its openness to questioning, to reimagining and to centering issues beyond nationalism, such as the environment, all in a context where the existence of a nation is precarious at best. Yet art insists on the luxury of nuance and the right to imagine the world otherwise, despite the bleakness of the present. The impetus to keep questioning, reframing and creating despite decades of genocide, erasure, displacement and the international community's abandonment of Palestine is something I want to honor in this book by foregrounding this complexity and radical dreaming.

Palestinian Film from the *Naqsa* to Now

Although some Palestinian film production existed prior to the *Naqba* of 1948, the first real flourishing of Palestinian film corresponded broadly with the period of Third Cinema globally: movements rooted in rejecting colonial or neocolonial structures that saw film as a tool of education and mass persuasion and were critical of Hollywood, its modes of film production and the ideological implications of film language rooted in this dominant paradigm.[15] This related period in Palestinian cinema, which Nurith Gertz and George Khleifi refer to as "The Third Period: Cinema in Exile, 1968–1982," included films largely made in neighboring Arab countries, where Palestinians were forced to take refuge, and under the auspices of various Palestinian revolutionary organizations. The Third Period began in the aftermath of Israel's 1967 attack (known as the *Naqsa*, or "disaster") and the illegal occupation of the West Bank, Gaza, the Golan Heights and the Sinai Peninsula. The *Naqsa* resulted in even more Palestinian displacement and the eventual relocation of the Palestinian Liberation Organization (PLO) to Lebanon from Jordan. The films of this period emerged after the relative absence of Palestinian cinema between the *Naqba* of 1948 and the *Naqsa* of 1967. Third Period films, made with support from organizations such as the PLO and others working under its umbrella, were made in service of the revolution. They foregrounded the plight of Palestinians and worked as tools of consciousness raising and mobilization. The films were almost exclusively documentaries, which addressed topics such as the plight of Palestinian refugees or Israeli oppression and the ongoing Palestinian resistance. *Our Small Houses*, the film that Alsharif marks over in *O, Persecuted*, is solidly located within this period of Palestinian film. It is worth quoting Gertz and Khleifi at length here on this period of cinema, since it provides a strong contrast with the work I discuss in what follows, much as Alsharif's body physically stages this relationship in *O, Persecuted.* Gertz and Khleifi note that the traumas of the *Nakba* and the *Naqsa* thereafter became unifying events in the articulation of a Palestinian identity that in reality was quite diverse before the violent establishment of the state of Israel:

> The narrative of trauma functioned as a unifying adhesive that enabled cinema to overcome controversies and differences . . . thus creating one history revolving around a single memory and shared by all. While this cinema blurred differences between genders, social strata, geographical areas, and generations within Palestinian society, it retained patriarchal stances that identified the homeland with masculinity. . . . Palestinian cinema strove toward the crystallization of a national, homogenous unity and created collective symbols that replaced the reality, heterogeneity, and diversity of Palestinian society.[16]

In what they call the Fourth Period, which begins where the Third ends and continues to the present of their book (2008), while some changes occur (notably the emergence of consistent narrative feature film production), the continued instability of Palestinian experience and the ongoing *Nakba* meant that many films continued to harbor an investment in the kind of nation-building on film that leaves less room for the modes of radical questioning or reimagining we see in the films I focus on here. As Gertz and Khleifi note of much Fourth Period cinema, specifically that made between the two Intifadas:

> It relied on a mythical past and the homogeneous national story—on symbols that arrest time and ignore the changes it brought with it, reviving the past in the present and reducing the diversity of Palestinian society to a homogenous representation.[17]

Whatever the strategic necessity of this kind of filmmaking has been for Palestinian filmmakers, the films I analyze here move away from nationalist rhetoric and fictions of homogeneity and attempt to reframe the Palestinian situation in all its impossibility and radical potentiality. These films deploy decolonial aesthetics that refuse to conceptualize politics as a teleological progression to exclusionary forms of statehood and that reconsider temporality, the ecosystem and other aspects of our being together from non-dominant, Palestinian perspectives.

Post-Third-Worldism and Decoloniality

The group of filmmakers discussed here aligns with what Ella Shohat has labeled "Post-Third-Worldist": no longer invested in maintaining a fiction of the unitary revolutionary nation, the work of Post-Third-Worldist filmmakers explores identities that fracture the "masculinist contours" of the nation, including those of women, and sexual and ethnic minorities.[18] The Post-Third-Worldist framework is complicated by the essentially stateless position of Palestinians, who do not create in response to or within a stable nation-state. Unlike many of the filmmakers Shohat references then, Palestine's future as a nation-state has yet to be determined. Furthermore, the settler-colonial nature of the Zionist project means that in many ways Palestine exists between the so-called Fourth and Third Worlds, fighting for a form of self-sovereignty whose spirit may not always align with the modernist/colonial construction of the nation-state. Above, I referred to this work as operating in post-nationalist modes. What I am reaching for here is an insistence on Palestinian sovereignty, as a group of people who have historical claim to a territory, while at the same time troubling the legitimacy of the concept of the nation-state as an entity tied to the legacy of colonial modernity and premised on exclusionary rhetoric and practices. As Steven Salaita teaches, when he refers to the nation, he is not referring to the nation-state but rather to the concept of the nation from an indigenous perspective, "as composed of heterogeneous communities functioning as self-identified collectives attached to particular land bases."[19]

Contemporary Palestinian art practices that direct their energies somewhere other than the nation-state are well-documented. Nayrouz Abu Hatoum, exploring Palestinian futurity through ethnographic analysis, observes that her case studies "reject the state as a constitutive figure" and reveal the "abandonment of a statist future or a rejection of a future that is made legible only through the imagination of a Palestinian state."[20] Yet she insists that her "interest in non-statist, non-national and non-spectacular forms of imagining the Palestinian future is not an invitation to abandon national and political forward-looking or forward-dreaming of a national destiny of Palestinian self-determination."[21] Similarly, the films I discuss here don't privilege the telos of the revolutionary nation-state in their exploration of Palestinian identity. In Sansour and Manna's work, questions of sustainability and ecological survival are inextricable from their politics. Issues of cultural plurality and gender equality also assume prominent positions in the visions of Palestine they offer. Alsharif makes a strong claim for transnational solidarities across forms of historical oppression and settler colonialisms, foregrounding something more broadly connective about Palestinian experience and dismantling the construct of borders, while questioning the ability of the nation-state to do justice to all of its people.

Many Palestinian filmmakers respond, as do the Post-Third-Worldist filmmakers Shohat discusses, to constructions of the nation that privilege a heteromasculinist conception, but in the case of Palestine, these filmmakers are not waiting for statehood to be achieved before they begin the work of decolonizing. Mona Hatoum's *Measures of Distance* (1988) is a foundational example of this challenge to heteromasculinist constructions of national identity. *Measures* is a meditation on the artist's distance from her mother and, by extension, her cultural origins. Hatoum reads letters that have crossed the distance from Beirut to London, the Arabic writing a transparent veil over photographs of her mother's naked body, while the audio track is an English translation, read by Hatoum herself. At one point, these translations across distance and language are interrupted altogether by the black screen of war. Meanwhile, in Lebanon, Hatoum's father raises controversy over the photographs of his wife taken by their daughter, posing questions about understandings of the female body, its proper place and to whom it belongs. *Measures of Distance* is a meditation on absence and dispersal, on war and the difficulties of communication across the borders and languages that shape diasporic experience, and it refuses to downplay questions of gender in order to paint a fully unified portrait of the exiled Palestinian family.

Mahasen Nasser-Eldin's *The Silent Protest: Jerusalem 1929* (2019) takes another approach in its examination of women's relationship to Palestinian identity and self-sovereignty. As the title indicates, the film (and filmmaker, who is visibly researching throughout the film) excavates a moment of formation for the Palestinian women's movement under British Mandate Palestine in 1929. Concerned about the influx of Zionists to Palestine and mistrustful of their designs on the territory, 300 women from around Palestine came together to protest the British Mandate government's support of the Zionists during the Buraq Uprising.[22] They write, "We have decided to carve a space for ourselves in the public sphere because we are half the nation. If not all the nation!" The film places the historical event in dialogue with the present by reading the protesters' documents while showing images of the contemporary landscape. Many of these shots center women and girls as they go about their daily lives or walk in groups. Like the women, who were forced to "march" via a convoy of cars because the government denied their request to walk in the streets, the filmmaker also shoots much of her footage from a moving vehicle. Of course, her method of documentation could also be due to the severe restrictions on Palestinian cultural production. These contemporary images and their mode of production thus constantly invite us to see the reality of the present in relation to former political aspirations. The film, like the work of Jumana Manna I discuss in the following chapter, turns to a pre-Israel, pre-*Nakba* period to foreground a moment of resistance and emergence. Historical photos of the women's group pepper the film, their images reflecting their modernity and sophistication. These women provide a very different reference point to the female *fedayeen* of the 1960s–80s. An alternate origin of feminist resistance is articulated throughout, and the film pointedly names the female martyrs of the period: the filmmaker informs us that "There were also two women on the list of unknown martyrs, whose identities remain unknown and excluded from history to this day." The gaps that haunt the present are reinforced through moments dedicated to the filmmaker's attempts to find the original house where the group of activists met and were photographed. Her struggle to locate the physical space speaks to the changes Palestine has suffered in the intervening years and the active erasure of Palestinian history. Yet in a truly Post-Third-Worldist vein, *The Silent Protest* not only offers an alternate image of women's political mobilization but also ponders whether this event was also a moment of misdirection. The women of 1929 state in their declaration:

> As we embark into the realm of political activity, we have to address serious considerations. Today we decided that the nation comes first and our women's liberation project comes second. We will liberate our land from colonial control and then we will form our national state through which we will gain our rights and equality as women.

These women, and Nasser-Eldin 90 years after them, foreground this strategic intersectional decision. The film ends with a series of questions: "What effects will these events and decisions have on future generations? Have we been fair to ourselves? Will we bear the burden of our decisions forever?" This moment in women's political history reverberates into the present to ask how current claims for Palestinian sovereignty entail various loyalties that may shape the future of Palestinian constructions of statehood or national identity.

Building on the Post-Third-Worldist framework, I use the term "decolonial," as opposed to postcolonial, throughout the text, in part because Palestine is not yet postcolonial in any sense of the word. Although decoloniality as a strategy applies to former colonies just as much as to the present settler colonies of Palestine/Israel and Turtle Island/North America, it functions differently and very practically in cases of settler coloniality, where sovereignty has not yet been achieved. In thinking about decolonial aesthetics, I am indebted to the work of Walter D. Mignolo, who argues that decolonial politics recognize the uneven-ness of "modernity"—that is, its emergence and values are inextricably linked to histories of imperialism and colonialism. Alternatives to modernity emerge when we delink modernity from its colonialist foundations: "A delinking that leads to a de-colonial epistemic shift and brings to the foreground other epistemologies, other principles of knowledge and understanding and, consequently, other economy, other politics, other ethics."[23] Decolonial aesthetics emerge from the colonized, offering alternative visions of the social, understandings of the natural world and ways of knowing. They may call into question the narrative of the nation-state as central to understanding identity. They may involve making connections across existing borders between social movements and struggles against dominant political orders. They advocate plurality over hierarchy in values and epistemic systems. Mignolo introduces the concept of trans-modernity, which "would be the overall orientation of de-colonizing and of delinking projects; an orientation toward pluri-versality as universal project leading toward a world in which many worlds will co-exist."[24] I see this impulse at work in Manna's documentaries and realized explicitly in Alsharif's *Ouroboros*.

Part of the decolonial process entails realizing the extent to which the values of heteropatriarchy are internalized by the colonized/occupied. In her book *Decolonial Queering in Palestine*, Walaa Alqaisiya charts the Zionist "hetero-conquest" of Palestine: "The Zionist desiring project gains its legitimacy through a naturalized account of gendered relations, presenting figures of the penetrator (masculinized) pioneer and the penetrated (feminized) native land, which also enables the marking of other bodies and desires as illegitimate."[25] Thus, regardless of Israel's hugely successful pinkwashing campaign, and of the individual identifications of Israelis within a gender/sexuality matrix, "settlers' inherent desire to spread their seeds and repopulate the land, construed as vacant, manifests the masculinist and heteronormative positionality of settler colonial violence in Palestine."[26] This discourse is mirrored in Palestinian nationalist visions of men as soldiers/martyrs and women as mothers of the (male) soldiers of the revolution, or as land to be fertilized. Rejecting this construction, a queer decolonial politics also refuses to see the colonizer as a savior figure, whose relative "modernity" can rescue the queer Palestinian from their own "backward" culture, and instead interrogates how colonial pinkwashing is internalized by the colonized culture. For the Palestinian, "queering is a struggle against those setter colonial power structures privileging patriarchy and heterosexuality, and thus hetero-colonialism."[27] Alqaisiya works with the queer Palestinian group alQaws, who beautifully articulate their queer decolonial politics. In one article alQaws writes:

> Queer liberation is fundamentally tied to the dreams of Palestinian liberation: self-determination, dignity, and the end of all systems of oppression. . . . Israeli settler colonialism, and tactics such as "pinkwashing" weaponize our queer experiences to place us in opposition to our own society and communities. Our answer to pinkwashing is to say that liberation is indivisible, and that there will be a place for all of us at the rendezvous of victory.[28]

The work of alQaws models in practice exactly what it looks like to assert equality in the midst of conditions of inequality and to radically imagine the society you strive for in a settler colonial context where any meaningful autonomy for Palestinians is yet to be realized. This commitment to complexity in the hope of creating a culture where all are free and included is a feature of the films I discuss here.

Ahlam Shibli's *Nine Days in Wahat al-Salam* (2010) also speaks to this in film form. It documents a nine-day workshop between Israeli Jews and Palestinians, all in their twenties and thirties. The workshop's goal is to foster dialogue around the current political impasse and for participants to "explore how Jews and Arabs can live together while each group maintains its uniqueness and identity." What particularly interests me about the film is that the director ends with an apology: a young Palestinian woman, Wafa'a, apologizes to a gay Israeli Jew, Ori, for dismissing his sexuality. On a previous day, Ori had claimed an identification as a "Palestinian Jew," but after feeling his sexuality was not accepted by the Palestinians in the working group, he felt less connection with Palestinians, and his belief in their ability to work together had been undermined. Waseem, a Palestinian participant, intervenes to say to Ori, "I am with you. No, I just wanted to say that." And others discuss the fact that perhaps Ori understands their experiences better because of his own marginalization. Wafa'a, however, dismisses Ori's sexuality as irrelevant to the question of statehood and a resolution to the occupation. She asserts that people have different morals, a use of terminology that obviously wounds Ori. On the workshop's final day, various participants offer their reflections on the process as a whole. Wafa'a apologizes to Ori, saying that she now realizes that when she said she didn't want to talk about his sexual identity, she was essentially saying she didn't want to talk about him. The fact that the film ends on this moment aligns with a Post-Third-Worldist refusal to put issues of ethnicity or nationalism above those of sexuality and inclusion. In fact, here the film seems to suggest that the full spectrum of our identifications is inseparable from learning how to live together and to work toward a society that is free from oppression.

Turning to the films I discuss in the following chapters, there are decolonial strategies at work throughout. Manna's decolonial practice at times invokes queer intertexts, foregrounds plurality as intrinsic to Palestinianness and restages less-visible narratives of Palestinian history. In Chapter 2, focusing on her films *A Sketch of Manners: Alfred Roch's Last Masquerade* (2013) and *A Magical Substance Flows into Me*, I explore how she draws from an alternative archive to represent Palestine as a melancholy and decadent costume party of anti-colonial Palestinians or as a space of musical, linguistic and ethnic plurality, where soundscapes reveal the mystical, yearning and joyful voices that populate the territory. Manna imagines Palestines that offer alternatives to patriarchal or heteronormative nationalisms. In Chapter 3, I focus on *Wild Relatives* and *Foragers*, documentaries that link her decolonial project to issues of food justice. The former film focuses on the global circulation of seeds, and the latter on Israel's ban on Palestinians foraging *'akkoub and za'atar*, greens central to their seasonal diet. Both films are instances of how Eric Ritskes describes decolonial practices in which "the conditions of possibility lie within the land and the reconfiguring of relationships through the land."[29] In the same vein, he argues that "Decolonization demands more than understanding the predatory modes of settler colonialism for resistance to them . . . but also the resurgence of alternative modes of being, alternative futures."[30] Manna's uses of countermapping and refusal as decolonial strategies call into question neocolonial understandings of agriculture and development, stage a rejection of settler colonial practices and offer alternative logics and relationships to the natural world.

In Chapter 4, I look at a group of Sansour's dystopian science fiction films: *A Space Exodus* (2009), *Nation Estate* (2012) and *In the Future They Ate from the Finest Porcelain* (2016), *In Vitro* and *As If No Misfortune Occurred in the Night* (2022). By removing questions of Palestinian identity from an explicit engagement with Israel as an entity within the diegeses of the films, Sansour generates representational spaces through which to imagine political setback and futurity outside of the frameworks and discourses that dominate thinking around Palestinian sovereignty. *In Vitro* stages larger questions of environmental collapse, memory and trauma, in ways that are both localized and much broader, transgressing the borders of the nation-state and challenging modernist teleologies. I frame her work in terms of Palestinian futurisms, derived from concepts such as Gulf- and Arab-futurisms and whose roots stem from the black radical traditions of Afrofuturism. Jussi Parikka notes that in Gulf Futurism there is a refusal "to reterritorialize modernity" or to tie "futurism to the nation state or any ethnicity in the post-Ottoman historical situation."[31] With respect to Sansour's and others' work, Lital Levy observes that "with the entrenchment of settler colonialism and fading actuality of a Palestinian state, Palestinian artists are producing work unbeholden to geographic and temporal borders."[32] In Sansour's films, Palestine acts as a microcosm and allows us to explore complex futures through the figures of Palestinian women. I return to this notion of Palestine as a microcosm below to argue for the larger relevance of these films to our historical moment. Parikka also speaks of the "temporal imaginaries" in the works he examines as "also ways to move horizontally, connecting different political struggles."[33] A horizontal movement connecting global struggles against oppression speaks to several of the works discussed here, but perhaps most specifically to Alsharif's *Ouroboros*.

In the films I discuss in the final chapter, *Ouroboros* and *Home Movies Gaza* (2013), Alsharif interrogates the dominant (neo)colonial visual frameworks for viewing Palestinians and rethinks space and time to undermine notions of modernity as linear progress. Her conceptually deft explorations of visuality under the occupation ask questions about how Palestinians are made to appear, while at the same time avoiding overdetermined images of suffering from the region, which have reduced Palestinian lives to a handful of visual tropes rooted in victimization and violence. Her work experiments with form and content, offering alternative conceptions of time and space that foreground connection, or what Mignolo would call transmodern histories that connect the oppressed and occupied across time and space. This tendency toward alternative temporalities and geographic unboundedness, particularly on display in *Ouroboros*, can also be linked to post-nationalist perspectives, well-described by Levy in relation to other Palestinian work: Levy notes that in this century, Palestinian cultural production has increasingly moved toward chronotopes rooted in "futurism, sci-fi, dystopia, environmental apocalypse, alternative histories, and cyclical timescapes."[34] I will speak about temporality throughout the book and the many decolonial forms it takes in these films, but I want to highlight here Levy's observations that "the temporality of post-1990s Palestinian literature and film has largely moved away from both the teleological time of political commitment and resistance and the theological time of certitude and forbearance"[35] and is "typically nonlinear, recursive, and disengaged from a military or political solution to Palestinian statelessness."[36] *Ouroboros* is the most radical of the films I discuss here in its exploration of time as a cycle and eternal return, as well as its fluid dance across borders, connecting Gaza to a world haunted by histories of violence that reverberate through the representation of the quotidian.

Palestine Is All of Us

In the "West," it now feels commonplace to claim a pandemic-related shift in our collective awareness that the world is changing in ways that aren't necessarily positive. We imagine ourselves to be grappling with a new world, shaped by the fear of the spread of infectious diseases, the fact that our access to basic resources can no longer be taken for granted, a sense of impending doom due to climate catastrophe and an uncertainty about how to move forward with the knowledge of the devastation we have wrought on the world and on each other. Art seems to be asking questions or seeking out imaginaries that address the need for hope in this dark time. For example, the international group exhibition *Twilight Land*, held at the Moderna Museet in Malmö in 2022–23 was framed in terms of

> the feeling of standing on the threshold of the unknown. Of realizing that our lives cannot continue in the same way—that things are in fact changing at a rapid pace—but not knowing what is to come. Feeling how the dominant story about life and the world is seriously skewed and realizing our dependence on a system that cannot last, while also experiencing how extremely difficult it is to think outside of this system and its story.[37]

Palestinian artists have for many generations lived in a post-apocalyptic moment, dispersed or under occupation, with little to no political hope after decades of political failure and a lack of meaningful international support. In the occupied territories, they live in a state of apartheid, with unreliable access to medical care, water, food and electricity (as I write this in the winter of 2024, while Israel is actively massacring Gazans, my language feels weak here). If some in the West are grappling with hopelessness, perhaps for the first time in their generation, we would do well to look to these filmmaker artists, who have been raised in a situation that has felt without hope, stagnant and empty, and yet have consistently revealed the power of art to reframe, reposition and reimagine in conceptually sophisticated ways that eschew any violent nationalisms or unitary positings of ethnic identity. From the poverty of reality are born acts of radical imagination that carry relevance far beyond the borders of Palestine.

In his book, *Global Palestine*, John Collins argues that Palestine bears "a relationship with the global that is both microcosmic and prophetic." The ways that colonization, securitization, acceleration and occupation are practiced against Palestinians both shape and show the earliest effects of the larger global dimensions of these violent processes.[38] But I want to build on Collins' discussion here: it is not only via the darker aspects of the testing and implementation of methods of domination, biopolitical or otherwise, that Palestine acts as a microcosm, but, returning to the question of what is next for us as humans, we can learn from the questions asked and the visions offered by these films to deeply rethink the values we've held sacred in the heart of empire.

Notes

1 Laura U. Marks, *Touch: Sensuous Theory and Multisensory Media* (Minneapolis: Minnesota University Press, 2002); Hamid Naficy, *An Accented Cinema: Exilic and Diasporic Filmmaking* (Princeton, NJ: Princeton University Press, 2001).
2 Both of these concepts have also been applied to the foundational text of diasporic Palestinian women's experimental video art, Mona Hatoum's *Measures of Distance* (1988).
3 Notable books that do contain some writing on Palestinian experimental filmmakers include Gil Z. Hochberg, *Visual Occupations: Violence and Visibility in a Conflict Zone* (Durham: Duke University Press, 2015) and Gil Z. Hochberg, *Becoming Palestine: Toward an Archival Imagination of the Future* (Durham: Duke University Press, 2021), as well as Laura U. Marks, *Hanan Al-Cinema: Affections for the Moving Image* (Cambridge: MIT Press, 2015).
4 Frantz Fanon, *The Wretched of the Earth* (London: Penguin, 1976), 183.
5 Kamran Rastegar, *Surviving Images: Cinema, War and Cultural Memory in the Middle East* (Oxford: Oxford University Press, 2015), 96.
6 Edward Said, *After the Last Sky: Palestinian Lives*, photographs by Jean Mohr (New York: Columbia University Press, 1999), 5.
7 Said, *After the Last*, 6, 20.
8 Greg Burris, *The Palestinian Idea: Film, Media, and the Radical Imagination* (Philadelphia: Temple University Press, 2019), 15.
9 Burris, *Palestinian Idea*, 54–55.
10 Burris, 58.
11 Burris, 29.
12 Burris, 58.
13 Said, 4.
14 Here I refer specifically to the Third Cinema-influenced PLO films post-1967 to 1982, what Gertz and Khleifi have called the "Third Period" of Palestinian cinema. Nurith Gertz and George Khleifi, *Palestinian Cinema:*

Landscape, Trauma, Memory (Bloomington: Indiana University Press, 2008).

15 *Nakba* (catastrophe) is the term for the forced displacement and mass murder of indigenous Palestinians with the establishment of the state of Israel in 1948. On Palestinian film history, see Gertz and Khleifi, *Palestinian Cinema.*

16 Gertz and Khleifi, 4.

17 Gertz and Khleifi, 6. Gertz and Khleifi make an exception for the work of Michel Khleifi, who they argue depicted a more diverse and less unified Palestine. The first Intifada or uprising occurred as mass resistance to Israeli occupation from within the territory between 1987 and 1993. The second Intifada occurred between 2000 and 2005. These both marked a significant shift from the location of Palestinian nationalism and resistance being based in countries outside of Israel/Palestine, such as Jordan and Lebanon, to being centered in the grassroots opposition of those living under active occupation.

18 Ella Shohat, "Post-Third-Worldist Culture: Gender, Nation, and the Cinema," in *Transnational Cinema: The Film Reader*, ed. Elizabeth Ezra and Terry Rowden (London; New York: Routledge, 2006).

19 Steven Salaita, *Inter/Nationalism: Decolonizing Native America/Palestine* (Minneapolis: University of Minnesota Press, 2016), *xiv*.

20 Nayrouz Abu Hatoum, "Decolonizing [in the] Future: Scenes of Palestinian Temporality," *Geografiska Annaler: Series B, Human Geography* 103, no. 4 (2021): 410.

21 Abu Hatoum, "Decolonizing," 401.

22 "The great Jewish demonstration organized by Zionist groups on August 15, 1929, at al-Buraq Wall/Western Wall of Al-Aqsa Mosque was the spark that ignited widespread clashes between Arabs and Jews in Jerusalem. It climaxed on August 23 and continued in the following days, punctuated by clashes between Arab demonstrators and the British army. The confrontations became known as the Buraq Uprising, during which 133 Jews were killed and 339 wounded, while 116 Arabs were killed and 232 wounded." "Al-Buraq Disturbance, 15–29 August, 1929," *The Interactive Encyclopedia of the Palestine Question, Institute for Palestine Studies*, August 12, 2021, www.palestine-studies.org/en/node/1651525.

23 Walter D. Mignolo, "Delinking: The Rhetoric of Modernity, The Logic of Coloniality and the Grammar of De-Coloniality," *Cultural Studies* 21, no. 2–3 (March–May 2007): 453.

24 Mignolo, "Delinking," 499.

25 Walaa Alqaisiya, *Decolonial Queering in Palestine* (London and New York: Routledge, 2023), 25.

26 Alqaisiya, *Decolonial Queering*, 25.

27 Alqaisiya, 8.

28 Quoted in Alqaisiya, 139.

29 Eric Ritskes, "Beyond and Against White Settler Colonialism in Palestine: Fugitive Futurities in Amir Nizar Zuabi's 'The Underground Ghetto City of Gaza,'" *Cultural Studies Critical Methodologies* 17, no. 1 (2017): 85.

30 Ritskes, "Beyond and Against," 79.

31 Jussi Parikka, "Middle East and Other futurisms: Imaginary Temporalities in Contemporary Art and Visual culture," *Culture, Theory and Critique* 59, no. 1 (2018): 49.
32 Lital Levy, "Temporalities of Israel/Palestine: Culture and Politics," *Critical Inquiry* 47 (Summer 2021): 693.
33 Parikka, "Middle East," 50.
34 Levy, "Temporalities," 676–77.
35 Levy, 691.
36 Levy, 691–92.
37 "Twilight Land," *Moderna Museet*, accessed December 15, 2023, www.modernamuseet.se/malmo/en/exhibitions/skymningsland/. It continues, "Naturally, the combination of an ecological and a geopolitical crisis worries and frightens. And in addition, the steady rise of authoritarian parties and movements has resulted in warnings of a twilight of democracy. At the same time, in the midst of this darkness, vibrant transition movements are engaging people all over the world and pointing in the direction of positive paradigm shifts—towards more life-affirming ways of thinking and living. We may find ourselves in a liminal state of instability, but it also inspires dreams and ideas about other worlds."
38 John Collins, *Global Palestine* (New York: Columbia University Press, 2011), 137.

Bibliography

Abu Hatoum, Nayrouz. "Decolonizing [in the] Future: Scenes of Palestinian Temporality." *Geografiska Annaler: Series B, Human Geography* 103, no. 4 (2021): 397–412.

"Al-Buraq Disturbance, 15–29 August, 1929." *The Interactive Encyclopedia of the Palestine Question, Institute for Palestine Studies*, August 12, 2021. www.palestine-studies.org/en/node/1651525.

Alqaisiya, Walaa. *Decolonial Queering in Palestine*. London; New York: Routledge, 2023.

Burris, Greg. *The Palestinian Idea: Film, Media, and the Radical Imagination*. Philadelphia: Temple University Press, 2019.

Collins, John. *Global Palestine*. New York: Columbia University Press, 2011.

Fanon, Frantz. *The Wretched of the Earth*. London: Penguin, 1976.

Gertz, Nuritz, and George Khleifi. *Palestinian Cinema: Landscape, Trauma, Memory*. Bloomington: Indiana University Press, 2008.

Hochberg, Gil Z. *Visual Occupations: Violence and Visibility in a Conflict Zone*. Durham: Duke University Press, 2015.

———. *Becoming Palestine: Toward an Archival Imagination of the Future*. Durham: Duke University Press, 2021.

Khalidi, Rashid. *The Hundred Years' War on Palestine: A History of Settler Colonialism and Resistance, 1917–2017*. London: Picador, 2020.

Levy, Lital. "Temporalities of Israel/Palestine: Culture and Politics." *Critical Inquiry* 47 (Summer 2021): 675–98.

Marks, Laura U. *Touch: Sensuous Theory and Multisensory Media*. Minneapolis: Minnesota University Press, 2002.

———. *Hanan Al-Cinema: Affections for the Moving Image*. Cambridge: MIT Press, 2015.

Mignolo, Walter D. "Delinking: The Rhetoric of Modernity, the Logic of Coloniality and the Grammar of De-Coloniality." *Cultural Studies* 21, no. 2–3 (March–May 2007): 449–514.

Moderna Museet. "Twilight Land." Accessed December 15, 2023. www.modernamuseet.se/malmo/en/exhibitions/skymningsland/.

Naficy, Hamid. *An Accented Cinema: Exilic and Diasporic Filmmaking*. Princeton, NJ: Princeton University Press, 2001.

Parikka, Jussi. "Middle East and other Futurisms: Imaginary Temporalities in Contemporary Art and Visual Culture." *Culture, Theory and Critique* 59, no. 1 (2018): 40–58.

Rastegar, Kamran. *Surviving Images: Cinema, War and Cultural Memory in the Middle East*. Oxford: Oxford University Press, 2015.

Ritskes, Eric. "Beyond and Against White Settler Colonialism in Palestine: Fugitive Futurities in Amir Nizar Zuabi's 'The Underground Ghetto City of Gaza.'" *Cultural Studies Critical Methodologies* 17, no. 1 (2017): 78–86.

Said, Edward. *After the Last Sky: Palestinian Lives*. Photographs by Jean Mohr. New York: Columbia University Press, 1999.

Salaita, Steven. *Inter/Nationalism: Decolonizing Native America and Palestine*. Minneapolis: University of Minnesota Press, 2016.

Shohat, Ella. "Post-Third-Worldist Culture: Gender, Nation, and the Cinema." In *Transnational Cinema: The Film Reader*, edited by Elizabeth Ezra and Terry Rowden, 39–56. London; New York: Routledge, 2006.

2 Ghosts and Echoes

Decolonial Historiography in the Films of Jumana Manna

Queering the Nationalist Text

Since her earliest short film *Blessed Blessed Oblivion* (2010), Jumana Manna's audiovisual work has refused to romanticize a unified notion of Palestinian identity. Her conceptually rich and politically powerful work encompasses film, sculpture and installation. She has turned her incisive gaze onto misogynist Palestinian subcultures, Israeli settler colonial policies and neocolonial eco-paternalism, among other subjects.

Blessed Blessed Oblivion is concerned with what are called "toxic" forms of masculinity: it explores a slice of muscle and car-obsessed Palestinian male "thug" culture in East Jerusalem. The film is a loose homage to Kenneth Anger's queer classic *Scorpio Rising* (1963), visually referencing *Scorpio's* framing and editing, with close-ups of work-worn hands caressing car parts, cigarettes dangling from mouths and well-gelled hair. Contemporary Arab pop music (and, memorably, Culture Beat's house hit "Mr. Vain") replace *Scorpio's* early 1960s pop soundtrack. Shots of men working on cars, lifting weights or visiting the barber shop reference the earlier film's bikers and fetishists (Figure 2.1). Both films explore forms of violent, rough masculinity: in *Oblivion*, the main subject (Ahmad) frankly discusses how he abused a devoted girlfriend. Complicating her outsider gaze, Manna, like Anger, is aware of her own desire shaping the film. At the outset of the film, we hear Ahmad tell dirty jokes over a black screen. Manna laughs, and he observes that she enjoys "this kind of talk." The ambivalence of desire colored by critique shapes the film—the imagery is erotic and playfully suggestive, while the snippets of dialogue included between song sequences reveal contradictions in the performance of thug masculinity as it intersects with ethnonationalist ideas. For example, in its final moments, the film returns to Ahmad, who finishes reciting a poem by Abd al-Rahim Mahmoud. This reference to the "martyr poet," who died fighting against Zionist forces in 1948, conjures a revolutionary nationalist history only to desacralize it. Ahmad recites a line from the poem declaring that he will defend his people with the sword and

DOI: 10.4324/9781003474449-2

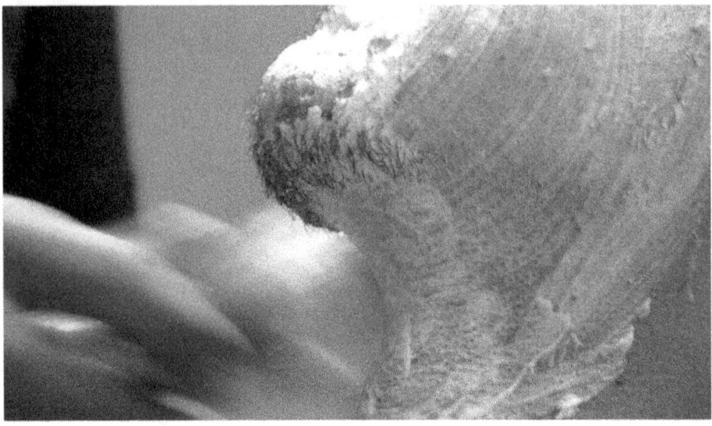

Figure 2.1 Blessed Blessed Oblivion (2010).

thus be recognized as male. He then explains, "Us Bedouins, we love to fuck! We cum like rivers. We ask the hand of your daughter Ksesa (little vagina), for our son Mizbir (big dick). The Sheikh Mityiz (ass) replied: Agreed! We give her to you open and ready for duty." The heteromasculine foundations of this iteration of Palestinianness are thus revealed as the reverent nationalist tone of the poem is juxtaposed with Ahmad's commentary on male virility and jokes about the exchange of women.

Manna's references to Anger's film queer the apparent heteronormativity of the misogynist milieu she explores. This queering gesture, alongside Manna's feminist gaze, offers a critique of these forms of Palestinian masculinity, particularly as they are linked to nationalism through Mahmoud's poetry. As noted in the introduction, this situates her work as "Post-Third-Worldist": she makes visible the asymmetries that structure particular conceptions of the nation, in this case heteropatriarchy.[1] In her work since *Oblivion*, Manna has continued to develop a vocabulary for representing the messy present, often through a critical engagement with the past. In this chapter, I explore the uses of history in her short film *A Sketch of Manners: Alfred Roch's Last Masquerade* (2013) and first documentary feature *A Magical Substance Flows into Me* (2017). The next chapter will look at Manna's turn toward a decolonial ecocritical mode of filmmaking in the nonfiction features *Wild Relatives* (2018) and *Foragers* (2022). Manna performs filmic countermappings in these more recent documentaries, privileging alternative narratives and imaginaries, in order to center urgent issues related to the growth and consumption of food as they intersect with geopolitics.

A Dandy in Jaffa: *Alfred Roch's Last Masquerade* (2013)

A Sketch of Manners: Alfred Roch's Last Masquerade is the first of Manna's two films that I discuss here in terms of their restaging of history to reframe the present. The short film unearths a fragment of a lost past, reactivating it in the present as a tableau vivant, by recreating an archival photograph of the last masquerade party thrown in Palestine by Alfred Roch (in 1942). Roch (1882–1942) was a member of the Palestinian elite and a political advocate for Palestinian sovereignty who fought against Zionist land appropriation.[2] I go into some detail about Roch's biography here because the issue of historical identification is central to how I situate these films. Jaffa's largest landowner (he specialized in the cultivation of its famous oranges), Roch attended school in Palestine and Lebanon and then studied agriculture in France. In 1902, an altercation with a group of Zionist settlers resulted in one of their deaths, and Roch had to leave Palestine because of the incident. He lived in Greece until he was able to return in 1908, due to the restoration of the Ottoman constitution. Again, in 1916, he was exiled to Anatolia, this time for his support of the Arab Revolt against the Ottomans, and returned to Jaffa at the end of the World War. He was politically engaged throughout the Three Year Revolt of 1936–39, a populist revolt against the British Mandate Administration that advocated both Arab independence and the end of British support for Zionist settlement and partition of Palestine.[3] During the revolt, Roch became a member of the newly created Arab Higher Committee.[4] In 1937, the British Mandate government disbanded the Arab Higher Committee and exiled many Palestinian leaders to the Seychelles.[5] However, this fate was avoided by Roch, who happened to be in Geneva at that time, advocating for Palestine at the League of Nations. He was unable to return to Palestine until 1942, the year of the photograph that inspired Manna's film. While in London in 1939, Roch spent his days as a political delegate for Palestine, while at night he attended the fabulous parties that he would recreate back home in Palestine, once allowed to return. Like Manna herself, Roch's life was spread across countries, suggesting an identificatory parallel through a shared diasporic status that also complicates ethnic homogeneity. In the film, Manna uses actors drawn from friends and family members, including her parents, further reinforcing the identification between the present and the past. Her strategic choice of figures of Palestinianness here is echoed in her first feature documentary (discussed next): they share a practice of historical unearthing and repetition through which we are asked to imagine particular Palestine*s* of the past in the present. Here, Manna chooses a figure of Palestinian resistance, but one temporally situated prior to the Nakba (as does Nasser-Eldin in *The Silent Protest* discussed in Chapter 1). As Palestinian identity is so rooted in and shaped by the trauma of the *Nakba*, it is noteworthy that she looks to a prior image of Palestinianness for her subject. In a similar vein, it is not the PLO figure of the revolutionary martyr she conjures but a cosmopolitan dandy, more exile than refugee. He is also a Roman Catholic, rather than a Muslim, a significant detail indicative of Manna's emphasis on plurality as intrinsic to Palestinianness, which we will see is also foregrounded in *A Magical Substance*.[6]

A Sketch of Manners opens with an image of post-party decadence. Roch lounges on a couch in an opulent room, still in his party costume and white make-up (Figure 2.2). A voiceover recites Baudelaire's poem, "A Former Life" (1857), accompanied by sounds of water dripping in a cave.[7] It cuts to Roch preparing for the party, while Caruso sings from *La Bohème* (a fitting commentary on Roch's lifestyle). Guests begin to arrive as the masquerade begins. Eventually, the film rests on a tableau vivant of the recreated photograph (see Figure 2.3). Throughout the film, a male voiceover speaking British English offers historical context, while the occasional cut away shows supporting archival images. The voiceover reproduces the authority and legitimacy of the standard documentary "voice of God," but not in order to critique this convention so much as to contextualize the images and validate them as historically meaningful. As the camera scans the tableau vivant, we hear diegetic sound: the awkward shuffling of the subjects trying to hold still adds a sense of anticipation laced with ennui to the scene. The diligent gaze of the camera documents each face in the crowd, its slow track burning a mnemonic imprint of the image into the spectator's mind. The final frames shift to the sound and imagery of water dripping in caves.

The cave evokes the past as fossil, residue, memory; it is referenced in the poem when Baudelaire says that the pillars of the portico where he lay "Seemed like basaltic caves when day expired." His description of how

Figure 2.2 Roch in repose.

Figure 2.3 The recreated photograph in *A Sketch of Manners* (2013).

perspective alters with time supports the film's reproduction of a Palestinian countermemory. Baudelaire's poem, treating memory, parallels the work of creative reconstruction that Manna performs, augmenting its tone of melancholy decadence. Baudelaire invokes his "slaves" (referencing his poems, according to common interpretation). He writes:

> Tended by many a naked, perfumed slave,
>
> Who fanned my languid brow with waving palms.
> They were my slaves—the only care they had
> To know what secret grief had made me sad.[8]

Manna suggests, by extension, that the photograph itself is a slave to her imagination, a melancholy site of identification with a lost Palestine and, more importantly, an *idea* of Palestine occluded in dominant rhetoric. The invocation of "slaves" also suggests both the relative privilege of Roch and the orientalist fantasies that shape Western representations of the East. Roch, while a colonial subject, remains part of an elite class, introducing an element of differentiation into the category of Palestinian that the film envisions. That the film's vision of Palestinian identity is resolutely not grounded in a fantasy of a homogenous historical Palestine is further reinforced by the queerness of the film: some guests are clearly in drag and camping it up. It is a party of mixed generations, mixed gender and sexual identifications, and mixed ethnicities (if, perhaps, shared class).

The poem's orientalist tones, layered over images of Palestinian decadence, intervene in the trope of the European traveler exoticizing what he sees in the East. Instead, it is the diasporic Roch who has traveled to Europe and borrowed freely, just as the film draws from French poetry to shape an image of Palestine. Hybridity and borrowing here are the norm, as are cultural differentiation and dynamism. The chosen archive is not grounded in a fantasy of cultural authenticity or pre-colonial purity, but yet it provides stubborn evidence of Palestinian *civilization*, of a resistance to colonialism and a strong independence movement alive and well prior to the Nakba. One review of the film reads *A Sketch of Manners* as critiquing the behavior of its subjects: "The performers recreate an early attempt at Western modernity, one that satirically portrays them as clowns."[9] But the film isn't primarily making fun of its subjects. The melancholy is too pervasive, and the film is too haunted by "secret grief" to be read as satirical. It does have a sense of humor: at one point, a servant briefly enters the frame and falls in a slapstick manner, just as the voiceover announces that "the Americans and the British were unprepared [for Germany's maneuvers]." But the film also celebrates the glamor and freedom of community that it showcases. Consider the title in this regard: it is a sketch of manners, that is, of the comportment of a certain class of society; but it is also *mannered*, a performance of identity, a masquerade, perhaps carrying tones of inauthenticity, but *contra* the film's reviewer here, not with the aim of satirizing their attempt at "Western modernity." This would imply a pure authentic Palestinianness that Manna believes in, and that hybridity, borrowing and play aren't central to all identities. In the film, identity feels less constraining for the moment, and there is a shared crossing over into fantasy and play, it is an instance of an explicitly *Palestinian* modernity. The image is haunted by the ghosts of history past and to come, but its reenactment reveals something of the generative performativity of identity that Homi Bhabha extolls:

> What is theoretically innovative, and politically crucial, is the need to think beyond narratives of originary and initial subjectivities and to focus on those moments or processes that are produced in the articulation of cultural differences. These 'in-between' spaces provide the terrain for elaborating strategies of selfhood—singular or communal—that initiate new signs of identity, and innovative sites of collaboration, and contestation, in the act of defining the idea of society itself.[10]

The photograph restaged in *A Sketch of Manners* reflects a moment of historical uncertainty: the devastation of 1948 is yet to come, and as the voiceover states, "The exhaustion from the three-year revolt had settled in the city. The Palestinian leadership was in jail or exiled to the Seychelles islands. The voice of the British mandate was fading, while the Great War continued elsewhere it seemed." Melancholy guests in black and white costumes gather under a colonial regime, indulging on the periphery of a World War, haunted by the ghosts of the past, as well as the *Nakba* to come (Figure 2.3). Roch himself died of a heart attack the year that the photo was taken, augmenting the image's ghostly nature. In their writing on decolonial practices in autoethnography, Eve Tuck and C. Ree center on the importance of listening to ghosts.[11] I deploy the term "haunting" methodologically here and not merely descriptively, drawing on Avery Gordon's work on hauntings as central to understanding modern social life, the workings of power and its constitutive absences: the ghost is the excluded figure, challenging the notion that everything in contemporary life is visible and introducing messiness and complexity into the picture of social reality.[12] As Gordon writes:

> The ghost is not simply a dead or a missing person, but a social figure, and investigating it can lead to that dense site where history and subjectivity make social life. . . . Being haunted draws us affectively, sometimes against our will and always a bit magically, into the structure of feeling of a reality we come to experience, not as cold knowledge, but as a transformative recognition.[13]

Haunting links the private and public, the individual and the social, and acts as a kind of diagnostic: what modes of power/knowledge are produced via particular narratives? Whose experiences are given visibility, and at what cost? As an alternative diagnostic, the purpose of invoking haunting "is to link the politics of accounting, in all its intricate political-economic, institutional, and affective dimensions, to a potent imagination of what has been done and what is to be done otherwise."[14] The ghost often exposes the violence of modernity: in the case of Palestine, the violence of its colonial past and present. The Palestinian landscape is filled with ghost towns, destroyed villages, cemeteries and orchards, renamed places and repurposed buildings, all haunted by their former uses, names and inhabitants. These ghosts speak to the violence of the past and ongoing colonial experience.

This haunting is at work in Razan AlSalah *Your Father Was Born 100 Years Old, and So Is the Nakba* (2017). The filmmaker uses Google Streetview to explore Haifa through the perspective of her (now deceased) grandmother, searching the streets for her lost son, Ameen. Her voice itself is ghostly, often as glitchy as the Google images of the city the cursor explores. Photos of Haifa before the *Nakba* are placed palimpsestically over the Google images, now dominated by Hebrew place-names and signage. Ameen's disappearance haunts the images, as do their former names, some Arabic and some reflecting British colonization. The grandmother comments, "One colonizing power made way to another." She narrates details about the past, which haunt the static Streetview images, saying, "There was a well here," or "They demolished 112 houses, one day after they forced us out. Today?! They've changed everything." She thinks she's discovered Ameen on a boat, taking the refugees to Lebanon, but is confused as to why tourists are there, taking pictures. Through her voice, the past is constantly present in the now of the immersive photos. Poetically, as the cursor explores a glitchy seascape, she notes that "Even the sea is broken."

When haunting is invoked in Manna's films, it unsettles the present by calling into being the violently excluded history of continuous Palestinian occupation of the land and produces new openings: if there are other pasts, there are other futures. Manna speaks with ghosts in order to produce counter-memories of Palestine and counteridentifications that challenge dominant discourses, both Israeli and Palestinian. They thus reveal how dominant narratives exclude particular productive images from the past: the ghosts of Palestinian possibilities. My invocation of Gordon's work resonates with Gil Hochberg's discussion of *A Sketch of Manners* and *A Magical Substance Flows into Me* as activating "minor archives" that ask us "to consider less familiar possibilities and configurations of the past and new ways of remembering, thereby opening new possibilities for imagining the future."[15] This reactivating of the past, such that the present is reframed and the future opens up to new narratives, is one of the magical functions that Roch's resurrection serves.

In both of the films I discuss in this chapter, Manna strategically chooses her archive so as to create a link, a historical identification, with a version of Palestine that is resilient and hopeful. Quoting Bhabha again on the fiction of an essential national or cultural identity, he writes:

> Social differences are not simply given to experience through an already authenticated cultural tradition; they are the signs of the emergence of community envisaged as a project—at once a vision and a construction—that takes you "beyond" yourself in order to return, in a spirit of revision and reconstruction, to the political *conditions* of the present.[16]

It is this focus on difference within Palestine and Palestinian-ness, not simply a challenging or reversal of colonial orientalist tropes, but a repurposing of history in the project of community, a politics of the present through an engagement with the past in all of its messiness, that these films perform.

Listening to Ghosts: *A Magical Substance Flows into Me* (2017)

Manna's first feature-length documentary *A Magical Substance Flows into Me* explores the diverse musical traditions of Palestine via the archives of Robert Lachmann, a German-Jewish ethnomusicologist. Lachmann's radio program (1936–38), produced for the Palestine Broadcasting Service while Palestine was under British Mandate, highlighted the ethnic diversity of the region through its musical traditions, including those of Kurdish and Yemenite Jews, Bedouins, Samaritans and Arab Palestinians. Lachmann came to Palestine fleeing the Nazi regime but never truly found a home there: although his papers and recordings are now kept in the national archive, he was unable to find a university position, and his radio program's lack of respect for the "boundaries" between Arab and Jew (I will return later to the figure of the Arab Jew) made him a controversial figure. *A Magical Substance* begins with a black screen, over which we hear Lachmann's voice (in 1936) petitioning those who have objected to the mix of Arab, Jewish and other ethnic traditions on the program. In English, he asks the broadcasting committee how he should proceed, given the "ill-feeling and insulting criticism" he has received from both Jewish and Arab listeners. Lachmann's archive challenges the notion of pre-1948 Palestine as a "land without people," while also highlighting the diversity of its inhabitants prior to the establishment of the state of Israel. Manna loosely recreates Lachmann's broadcasts in the film, recording musicians who have maintained the various musical traditions to the present. The film is comprised of these interviews and musical performances (interspersed with footage of Manna's parents) and images of Lachmann's archival photographs and handwritten lectures, read by Manna herself in voiceover. In its restaging of the past in the present, the film destabilizes the Israeli state's attempt to enforce a homogenous national identity through the replacement of diverse language traditions with Hebrew and by suppressing diverse ethnic cultural practices in favor of identification with the nation-state. The film thus cycles back to the past to echo or repeat it in the present, challenging Israeli ethnonationalism while also insisting on the plurality of culture in present-day Israel/Palestine.

Indicative of the film's perspective, the song played over the opening title is "Linda" (1983), sung by Haim Moshe, an Arab-Jewish musician of Yemenite background. Moshe is credited with helping Israeli Mediterranean or "Mizrahi" music, which had been largely ignored or ghettoized by mainstream Israeli culture, achieve mainstream acceptance. The use of Arabic lyrics, scales and other "Eastern" influences in Mizrahi music did not align with the Eurocentric tastes of the Ashkenazi Jews, whose preferences shaped the state-building music known as *Shirey Erez Yisrael* ("Songs of the Land of Israel").[17] The music of Arab Jews asserted other cultural traditions with deeper roots than that of the new nation and signified a failure to fully assimilate to the hegemonic paradigm, further marginalizing them within the new state. Moshe's "Linda" exploded in popularity with Arab audiences in Lebanon, Jordan, Syria and even within the occupied territories. The hybridity and transnational appeal of the music of Moshe and other Mizrahi-Jewish musicians are emblematic of the messiness and complexity of identity that Manna refuses to smooth over in her film. This is particularly ironic given Lachmann's own orientalist-inflected search for "authentic" and "pure, unspoiled" musical traditions.

Despite their differences, in her choice of Lachmann as ghostly muse, Manna is intentionally turning to a marginal history, or a "minor archive," to borrow from Hochberg. Lachmann died in 1939, four years after coming to Palestine, his project never fully accepted by Arabs or Jews. According to

Manna's description, Lachmann was also gay, a sexual outsider. As in her previously discussed films, a queering of the national text seeps in, this time through Lachmann as a gay pluralist. The film notably does not resurrect a historical fantasy of ethnic homogeneity but reveals a Palestine where many different people live together with deep-rooted and valuable cultural traditions.

Manna physically appears near the film's beginning. Her presence is indicative of how she positions herself as a documentarian/author in the work. The film's first visit is to a Kurdish Jew. His son tells Manna in the elevator ("Isralift") up to the apartment that his father might not perform in his police costume: he rarely wore it because he was assigned to security duties in the occupied territories. Once in the apartment, the father grills Manna on her parents' occupations and their feelings toward her work. This dialogue allows her to situate herself in terms of gender, class and ethnicity: the professional class of her parents is revealed (her father is a professor, and her mother directs a program for teachers of early childhood education), and the tensions around her position as a young female Palestinian artist conducting research in primarily male-dominated and ethnically divergent spaces are made evident. Manna attends Shabbat dinner in the man's home, and he discovers in talking with her that "they" (i.e., Arabs) have the same word for *mkhalal* (pickled turnips) that is used in Hebrew. In addition to showcasing Manna's linguistic flexibility and cultural hybridity, these scenes highlight the complexity of her Arab non-Jewish presence at the Shabbat dinner of someone who earned a living enforcing the illegal occupation. At the same time, they suggest the possibility of cultural exchange and connection, revealing the politics of her vision of Palestinian futures.

In her discussion of *A Magical Substance*, Hochberg characterizes the film as "a metacinematic engagement with the question of historical potentiality, the mobility of the archive, and the ability to capture a futurity that, while dependent on the past, is also unpredictable in its evolution and configurations."[18] She observes that the figure of the Arab or Mizrahi Jew is central to the film's construction: minutes 21:55 to 30:00 of the film's roughly 66 minute running time are concerned with interviewing and documenting the music of Neta Elkayam, a singer of Moroccan Jewish ancestry (Figure 2.4). Elkayam sings in her kitchen as she prepares food and discusses her family's migration to Israel. She describes how part of her grandmother always remained back in Morocco, actively seeking out the Arabs in the new neighborhood and persisting as a stubborn counter-presence to her assimilating children. As Elkayam grew up, she began to question the version of identity that her parents and the Israeli state transmitted, wondering why she had been required to give up familial and cultural traditions with much deeper roots. For Hochberg, Elkayam is a figure of hybridity that illustrates Manna's refusal to offer a tidy version of what Palestine is or will be. I would add to this that she is, significantly, the only female musician in the film. One thing that the many traditions documented in the film share is a patriarchal

Figure 2.4 Neta Elkayam in *A Magical Substance*.

system of transmission. Whatever the differences in religious beliefs or cultural practices that the film observes, women's marginalization with respect to musical practices and sacred/social spaces seems to connect them. We see the all-male religious gathering of the Samaritans early in the film, for example, and the all-male social space of the Bedouins sometime later. Manna subtly draws our attention to gender through her camera's attention to the wives of various musicians in the film (Figure 2.5). She captures these women working in their kitchens while their husbands are being interviewed or listening to Lachmann's broadcasts; she is curious about their thoughts on the music and their own histories. In one telling incident, the Samaritan elder, listening to Lachmann's recording, calls out to his wife in the kitchen, "Im Wasif, come and hear your father's voice. Come." She responds, "But I don't know him." When the couple finally sit together in front of the camera, they begin speaking at the same time: he blurts out regarding the recording, "This is treasure," while his wife says, "I used to hear about him. My mother . . . he left my mother when she was twenty-two years old." Im Wasif goes on to note that her mother bore him six children, three boys and three girls. The tension between their perspectives reveals concerns shaped by gender segregation; where *he* marvels at the quality of the paternal voice, *she* hears only abandonment and neglect.

In another instance, near the film's end, a Palestinian *shabbaba* maker's daughter sits on the steps playing a toy mouth organ. The camera lingers on her at length, suggesting another possible route of transmission for this music

Figure 2.5 A Magical Substance Flows into Me (2017).

(Figure 2.6). Returning to Neta Elkayam, it is significant, then, that she sings in her kitchen as she cooks. She bridges the activity of the many women seen busying themselves with the reproduction of life and culture in the kitchen with the power of music as another tool of cultural transmission and reproduction. It is here again that we see Manna's "Post-Third-Worldism," not only challenging Israel's cultural and discursive hegemony but also opening up a space for thinking about women's contributions to Palestinian futures.

Manna's use of her own parents provides a counterpoint to the many homes and workplaces we visit in the film that display more conventional gender roles. Manna uses her parents throughout her work: they are two figures in the tableau vivant of *A Sketch of Manners*, and they are featured in the more recent *Foragers*. Manna grew up in an educated, economically stable and modern nuclear family, and this shapes the landscape of how she constructs Palestinianness in her work. An early shot lingers outside of her parents' kitchen window. Her mother (Aziza) tells her father (Adel) to take out the compost and mentions a pan that needs to be washed. This brief snippet of dialogue suggests a degree of shared domestic labor. Aziza is shown doing yoga several times in the film, and Adel, a historian, offers the camera historical anecdotes about Zionism and the Nakba. The use of Manna's own parents is significant in terms of the film's focus on lineage and transmission. They disrupt any stereotypical notions of Arabness and offer a picture of a Palestinian present that is neither archaic nor parochial. Although her parents are not musicians, they help to situate the subject behind the camera in relation to

Figure 2.6 The daughter of the *shabbaba* maker as a future musician.

what is shown onscreen. At one point, while telling a story about his Iraqi Jewish friend from the gym, her father puts on an Umm Khoultum cassette and sings along to "You Oppress Me" as he makes coffee. Again, a female voice enters the soundscape.

In her writing on feminist historical methodology, Joan Wallach Scott develops the concept of the *fantasy echo*. The term derives from a student's mis-hearing of the French term *fin-de-siècle*, but Scott finds this malapropism useful for thinking about the way in which an identity is discursively invoked—and thereby constructed—across times and places. In the case of "woman" or "women," Scott argues that any invocation of a link between women across time and space is predicated on a fantasy that the term "woman" signifies the same thing in, say, 19th-century India, 15th-century Italy and 21st-century France. The process of historical writing is performative, in that categories such as woman are brought into being rhetorically: the connections we make across history are fantasy echoes that retrospectively form our understanding of the past while shaping what the category signifies in the present. Scott explains:

> Identities don't preexist their strategic political invocations, . . . categories of identity we take for granted as rooted in our physical bodies (gender and race) or our cultural (ethnic, religious) heritages are, in fact, retrospectively linked to those roots; they don't follow predictably or naturally from them.[19]

This is useful for understanding Manna's historical reckoning with her elective archives. They are a strategic engagement with a chosen understanding of what Palestine and Palestinian-ness are and have been. As Homi Bhabha argues, "Terms of cultural engagement, whether antagonistic or affiliative, are produced performatively. The representation of difference must not be hastily read as the reflection of *pre-given* ethnic or cultural traits set in the fixed tablet of tradition."[20] If, after Scott and Bhabha, we see Palestine or Palestinian identity not as an essentialized given but rather as "a rhetorical political strategy invoked differently by different [Palestinians] at different times," we gain insight into the historiographical strategy and politics of these films.[21] This is by no means a depoliticizing of cultural identity: Manna's work is definitively political, challenging the settler colonial Israeli regime and, as we will see in the next chapter, international practices of paternalist neo-colonialism. Palestinian culture and history emerge as central to Manna's filmmaking, but never in an essentialist or ethnonationalist mode. Hybridity, mutability, connection through food and music and the contributions of women all work to rhetorically invoke Palestine<u>s</u> that reject potentially violent and masculinist ethnic frameworks.

Roch and Lachmann, Manna's "ghosts," are strategically chosen retrospective identifications or "fantasy echoes." This is not to say that Lachmann is a representative of Palestinianness per se, but his research, despite its Orientalist timbre, offers an opportunity for imaginary engagement—a version of Palestine that can be invoked in the present, in the interest of what Palestine can signify in the future. That Lachmann is a figure of identification for Manna is evidenced not only by the way in which she follows his footsteps in the present but also through her use of his broadcasts and lectures within the film. It is she who plays the recordings of his radio program for the various musicians she interviews, acting as an intermediary or stand-in for Lachmann in the present. Furthermore, she reads his lectures throughout the film. Her voice, reading Lachmann's words in English, creates an identificatory link while also recoding the voice of authority as female in the present. Beyond identification, Manna's voicing of Lachmann's lectures claims an authorial perspective on largely male traditions. The fact that the text is in English speaks to the impurity that has long existed in Palestine, histories of colonial rule replaced by settler colonialism. It also invokes Lachmann and Manna's diasporic experiences, from which stem their linguistic competencies. The degree to which Lachmann's politics or vision align with Manna's in the present is not important if we deploy the notion of the fantasy echo to understand Manna's historical engagement with the musicologist. As Scott says, "Retrospective identifications, after all, are imagined repetitions *and* repetitions of imagined resemblances."[22] Manna's work is so rich because she not only invokes the identification but at the same time she historicizes the differences between past and present, rather than eliding them, performing the work of the critical historian. For example, in the introduction to Elkayam's segment, we hear Lachmann's lecture (read by Manna) regretting that he has to rely on recordings for an episode on North African Jewish music, rather than collaborating with live musicians, "But the particular types of music I want to show you are not practiced in Palestine." The interview with and performance of Elkayam reveal the impact of the Israeli state on the demographics of the region, bringing in Arab Jews from the Maghreb and the Asian continent. *A Magical Substance* represents this change as a positive failure in the present: what was meant to bolster the Zionist settler colonial project ultimately reveals and deepens fractures in the ideological basis of Israel. "Hybridity intervenes in the exercise of authority not merely to indicate the impossibility of its identity but to represent the unpredictability of its presence."[23] Manna's vision challenges the idea that issues of hybridity, so foregrounded in the postcolonial canon, are not relevant to Palestine.[24] An Arab voice sings in Arabic, and the "Mizrahi Jew" (a term that replaces Arab with *Mizrahi*, a word meaning "Eastern" and that erases specific countries of ancestral origin) insists on her Arab identity and Moroccan roots. Here, the differences between Lachmann's Palestine and Palestine today expose not only histories of violence but also the plurality and cultural enrichment that define the film's vision of Palestine.

In thinking about difference and identification, Bhabha is again useful in dialogue with Scott: "The recognition that tradition bestows is a partial form of identification. In restaging the past it introduces other, incommensurable cultural temporalities into the invention of tradition."[25] Manna shares Bhabha's vision of culture as plural and dynamic and the nation as a project whose finality or totality is always undermined by its minorities, its victims and its exclusions. Manna's films queer forms of historical identification and center gender, in addition to emphasizing religious and ethnic pluralism.

Another way we might engage with the complexity of historical identification here is via the contrast between the speech of Lachmann, voiced by Manna, and the images that the film chooses as a counterpoint to his lectures. As Stephanie van der Peer notes in her book *Negotiating Dissidence: The Pioneering Women of Arab Documentary* (van der Peer is referencing Stella Bruzzi's writing on documentary), "The very presence of a female voice tampers with the unity and the universality of the male voice-over spectators are used to: it creates a critical distance."[26] The critical distance is reinforced by Manna's control of the images. When Lachmann uses dry and objectifying academic prose, Manna shows an image of one camel drinking another camel's urine. Lachmann discusses Kurdish religious music in mystical terms, noting that the liturgical music "goes back to prehistoric conditions of life." He writes that

> the cult lay in a magical ceremony intended to attract benefit to and dispel misfortune from the respective community. The sorcerer, or the medicine man of the tribe, works himself into a trance by means of intoxicants and

> bodily movements. In this state, the voices of demons speak through him. We must not imagine that this ceremony, in spite of low standard of civilization, is wild and unorganized. From the magical point of view, nothing short of scrupulous precision can achieve the desired effect of the ceremony.

This text is accompanied by footage of the decidedly uninspiring land assessment office where the Kurdish musician works. With fluorescent lighting and stock imagery on the walls, the frumpy men sitting behind computers or hunched awkwardly over paperwork offer a banal counterpoint to Lachmann's language of demons and magic; here, the "scrupulous precision" of the ceremony operates in a more administrative realm. But these banal images also reverberate with the violence of the present: maps on the office wall reference the taking of land from Palestinians and the expansion of Israeli settler colonialism (e.g., one poster is labeled "Table of land expropriation according to plan 4558"). These moments reveal the film's distance from and reframing of the source material to historicize difference and offer a Palestinian (and feminist) perspective on the present via the past.

A Magical Substance depicts a territory where diverse populations coexist within a state committed to the violent erasure of many, where women are instrumental to the transmission of culture and where a gay refugee's radio show provides an alternate point of entry into the history of a place. This is not a Palestine rooted in a fantasy of unity or homogeneity, nor does it work to suture the cracks within the present. *A Magical Substance* ends with the joyous performance of a Palestinian *dabke*. Three men perform an infectious song, while a fourth emerges, apparently spontaneously, to dance along for the camera. They play in a humble garage, a clothesline resting on the keyboardist's shoulder. Despite the brutal reality of their political context, it is a moment of happiness, community and cultural transmission. The little girl who plays the mouth organ briefly enters the frame.

Notes

1 Ella Shohat, "Post-Third-Worldist Culture: Gender, Nation, and the Cinema," in *Transnational Cinema: The Film Reader*, ed. Elizabeth Ezra and Terry Rowden (New York; London: Routledge, 2006).

2 My information on Roch is from "Alfred Roch," *Interactive Encyclopedia of the Palestine Question*, accessed August 1, 2023, www.palquest.org/en/biography/25367/alfred-roch.

3 For more on the revolt, see Rashid Khalidi, *The Hundred Years' War on Palestine: A History of Settler Colonialism and Resistance, 1917–2017* (London: Picador, 2020), 42–49.

4 According to Khalidi, "The AHC tried to take charge of the general strike, but unfortunately their most important achievement was to broker an end to it in the fall of 1936 at the request of several Arab rulers, who were

essentially acting at the behest of their patrons, the British," *The Hundred Years' War on Palestine*, 43.

5 The British Mandate Government's response to the revolt went well beyond the exile of leaders: Khalidi refers to the "refinements of callousness and cruelty employed" in the suppression of Arab resistance via a "bloody war . . . which left 14 to 17 percent of the adult male Arab population killed, wounded, imprisoned, or exiled," *The Hundred Years' War on Palestine*, 44.

6 As noted in "Alfred Roch," "on 20 August 1936, Roch was one of the signatories to a statement made by leaders of the Christian community in Palestine, in which they appealed to the Christian world to save [Christian] holy sites from the Zionist threat and drew the attention of Christians all over the world to the danger posed by British policy, which supported the Zionist project, to the future of Palestine."

7 The full text of the poem is here:

> Long since, I lived beneath vast porticoes,
> By many ocean-sunsets tinged and fired,
> Where mighty pillars, in majestic rows,
> Seemed like basaltic caves when day expired.
>
> The rolling surge that mirrored all the skies
> Mingled its music, turbulent and rich,
> Solemn and mystic, with the colours which
> The setting sun reflected in my eyes.
>
> And there I lived amid voluptuous calms,
> In splendours of blue sky and wandering wave,
> Tended by many a naked, perfumed slave,
>
> Who fanned my languid brow with waving palms.
> They were my slaves—the only care they had
> To know what secret grief had made me sad.
>
> F. P. Sturm, "A Former Life," in *Baudelaire: His Prose and Poetry*, ed. Thomas Robert Smith (New York: Boni and Liveright, 1919), 147.

8 Sturm, "A Former Life," 147.

9 Daryl Meador, "Arab Spring Meets Warhol in Ramallah Show," *The Electronic Intifada*, December 4, 2012, https://electronicintifada.net/content/arab-spring-meets-warhol-ramallah-show/11967.

10 Homi K. Bhabha, *The Location of Culture* (London; New York: Routledge, 1994), 2.

11 Eve Tuck and C. Ree, "A Glossary of Haunting," in *Handbook of Autoethnography*, ed. Stacy Holman Jones, Tony E. Adams, and Carolyn Ellis (Walnut Creek: Left Coast Press, Inc., 2013).

12 Avery Gordon, *Ghostly Matters: Haunting and the Sociological Imagination* (Minneapolis: University of Minnesota Press, 1997).

13 Gordon, *Ghostly*, 8.

14 Gordon, 18.
15 Gil Z. Hochberg, *Becoming Palestine: Toward an Archival Imagination of the Future* (Durham: Duke University Press, 2021), 47.
16 Bhabha, *Location*, 4.
17 Amy Horowitz, "Israeli Mediterranean: Straddling Disputed Territories," *Journal of American Folklore* 112, no. 445 (Summer 1999).
18 Hochberg, *Becoming Palestine*, 45.
19 Joan W. Scott, "Fantasy Echo: History and the Construction of Identity," *Critical Inquiry* 27, no. 2 (Winter 2001): 285.
20 Bhabha, 3.
21 Scott, "Fantasy Echo," 286.
22 Scott, 287.
23 Bhabha, 168.
24 See, for example, Smadar Lavie and Ted Swedenburg, eds., *Displacement, Diaspora and Geographies of Identity* (Durham: Duke University Press, 1996).
25 Bhabha, 3.
26 Stephanie van der Peer, *Negotiating Dissidence: The Pioneering Women of Arab Documentary* (Edinburgh: Edinburgh University Press, 2017), 20.

Bibliography

"Alfred Roch." *Interactive Encyclopedia of the Palestine Question*. Accessed August 1, 2023. www.palquest.org/en/biography/25367/alfred-roch.

Bhabha, Homi K. *The Location of Culture*. London; New York: Routledge, 1994.

Hochberg, Gil Z. *Becoming Palestine: Toward an Archival Imagination of the Future*. Durham: Duke University Press, 2021.

Horowitz, Amy. "Israeli Mediterranean: Straddling Disputed Territories." *Journal of American Folklore* 112, no. 445 (Summer 1999): 450–63.

Khalidi, Rashid. *The Hundred Years' War on Palestine: A History of Settler Colonialism and Resistance, 1917–2017*. London: Picador, 2020.

Lavie, Smadar, and Ted Swedenburg, eds. *Displacement, Diaspora and Geographies of Identity*. Durham: Duke University Press, 1996.

Meador, Daryl. "Arab Spring Meets Warhol in Ramallah Show." *The Electronic Intifada*, December 4, 2012. https://electronicintifada.net/content/arab-spring-meets-warhol-ramallah-show/11967.

Peer, Stephanie van der. *Negotiating Dissidence: The Pioneering Women of Arab Documentary*. Edinburgh: Edinburgh University Press, 2017.

Scott, Joan W. "Fantasy Echo: History and the Construction of Identity." *Critical Inquiry* 27, no. 2 (Winter 2001): 284–304.

Shohat, Ella. "Post-Third-Worldist Culture: Gender, Nation, and the Cinema." In *Transnational Cinema: The Film Reader*, edited by Elizabeth Ezra and Terry Rowden, 39–56. London; New York: Routledge, 2006.

Sturm, F. P. *Baudelaire: His Prose and Poetry*. Edited by Thomas Robert Smith, 147. New York: Boni and Liveright, 1919.

Tuck, Eve, and C. Ree. "A Glossary of Haunting." In *Handbook of Autoethnography*, edited by Stacy Holman Jones, Tony E. Adams, and Carolyn Ellis, 639–58. Walnut Creek: Left Coast Press, Inc., 2013.

3 Decolonial Ecologies in Jumana Manna's *Wild Relatives* (2018) and *Foragers* (2022)

Film as Countermap

Jumana Manna's *Wild Relatives* (2018) and *Foragers* (2022) are documentaries rooted in decolonial ecologies. As filmic countermaps of sorts, they track flows of seeds and international aid and chart practices of land use. *Wild Relatives* moves primarily between the Bekaa Valley in Lebanon and the Svalbard Global Seed Vault in artic Norway, following the movement of seeds and bodies across borders. *Foragers* returns to Palestine, situating its drama in Jerusalem, the Galilee and the Golan Heights. Exploring the established cultural practice of foraging greens central to the Palestinian diet and cultural life, which the Israeli state has criminalized, the film juxtaposes the persecution of pickers with the Israeli commercial production of these same greens for sale to the captive Palestinian market. Both *Wild Relatives* and *Foragers* map the connections between people, agricultural practices and land use, situating these relationships within transnational neo- and settler colonial practices. They also avoid any explicitly ethnonationalist paradigm, instead prioritizing sustainability and the holistic relationship of people to each other and to the land.

Before discussing the documentaries, I will clarify some of the concepts that are central to how I am framing these films. Countermapping is a concept originating in the discipline of geography.[1] Connected to activism and advocacy, it realizes the potential of datamaps to challenge and reconfigure the way we see social, economic, environmental and other relations. Mapmaking has deep roots in imperialist and nationalist histories ("The history of mapmaking is also a history of colonization," an ongoing reality in Palestine), and maps are never, of course, neutral and objective records of the "real."[2] Countermapping harnesses the power of the map to "interven[e] in the world" and present alternative information that challenges dominant ways of understanding spaces and places.[3] For example, a map of the United States that highlights the proximity of historically black communities to superfund sites would make visible patterns of structural environmental racism.

Manna's films do not explicitly represent maps but work in a manner akin to the countermap, in that they follow practices and policies within and

DOI: 10.4324/9781003474449-3

between spaces to reveal the production of dependencies or how the law is instrumentalized to disenfranchise some and perpetuate inequalities. Sebastian Cobarrubias notes, "In geography, countermapping has most often been associated with questions and struggles over land use and conservation."[4] As we will see, struggles over land use are central to *Foragers* but are also poignantly relevant in *Wild Relatives*, as in the moment when a Lebanese landowner discusses the greater profitability of using his land for refugee camps instead of farming. Nick Gill et al., 2018 argue that "By 'following' phenomena such as food and minerals, the complexity, contradictions, and over-arching logics of their journeys can be laid bare."[5] In this vein, Manna's films explore how "everyday objects [are] linked to broader political-economic processes."[6] In these documentaries, the objects followed are seeds and greens, whose circulation cannot be separated from the humans who use them and who perpetuate and/or resist the political and economic context that determines their movement.

These countermaps are grounded in a decolonial environmental politics, but we cannot take for granted that an environmentally rooted perspective is inherently decolonial. As Ramachandran Guha argues in his takedown of the American deep ecology movement's imperialist tendencies, environmental perspectives that critique anthropocentrism as the problem, in favor of a shift toward biocentric models, obfuscate some of the major causes of the ecological issues facing the planet, namely, overconsumption by the First World (and by Third World elites) and, globally, increasing militarization.[7] Guha cautions against a global ecological stance, which can avoid a focus on "inequalities *within* human society" and how their production is connected to issues of land use and sustainability at a local level.[8] As Cara Cilano and Elizabeth DeLoughrey note, many Western ecological approaches evince orientalist tendencies, rendering "the nonwestern subject and landscape" "the *tabula rasa* upon which to inscribe the agency of the western ecologist."[9] By contrast, "a vital aspect of postcolonial ecocriticism refuses the nostalgia of pure landscape even while it grapples with the best ways of addressing the representation of the nonhuman environment."[10] While much of the literature I reference here uses the term "postcolonial," as noted in the first chapter, the settler colonial context is not "post." John Collins describes Israel's "war on the milieu," a concept that refers to the ways that Israeli strategy "has increasingly taken the form of a war that is waged directly on a people's capacity for biological and social reproduction and on the natural and built environment that ensures their survival."[11] This, of course, includes the most basic elements of life: "food, water, shelter, vegetation, education and infrastructure."[12] *Foragers* shows this war at work on Palestinians, and it is dramatically evident in the complete destruction of Gaza that is underway as I write in the fall of 2023, where it is unclear whether anyone (Palestinians or Israeli colonists) in the near future will be able to live a healthy, viable life in the environments of Gaza that the Israeli army has razed.

The global relations charted in *Wild Relatives* are neocolonial in nature, and the term "decolonial" better captures an actively oppositional representational practice that challenges the manufacturing of relations of dependence on the global north by so-called developing countries, as well as the struggle against settler colonial logics in *Foragers*. That said, the colonial structures made visible in the documentaries follow similar patterns to those elucidated in postcolonial representation and theory. Graham Huggan and Helen Tiffin observe that "One of the central tasks of postcolonial ecocriticism to date has been to contest western ideologies of development, but without necessarily dismissing the idea of 'development' itself as a mere tool of the technocratic west."[13] This perspective that critiques colonial constructions without reproducing geopolitical binaries of development versus underdevelopment is evident throughout *Wild Relatives*, which is replete with representations of Arab modernities. The film highlights the scientific and technical competence of the Arab team in Lebanon while simultaneously critiquing the policies and ideology that motivate the seed bank and, in part, have made its existence necessary. It also offers a powerful decolonial counterimage of development in the figure of a refugee farmer.

The Decolonial Eco-Politics of *Wild Relatives*

In focusing on the relationship between a site in Norway and Levantine countries, *Wild Relatives* reflects the time Manna spent studying in Norway and connects to her other projects focused on the relationship between Norway and Palestine, such as her 2013 short film *The Goodness Regime* (co-directed with Sille Storihle).[14] In this short experimental documentary, children reenact a series of events in the history of Norway, all of which contribute to the mythologization of Norway as a benevolent and peaceful nation. These scenes are interspersed with various genres of found footage that work to satirize and call into question the Norwegian national identity. The global seed vault, featured in *Wild Relatives*, is paradigmatic of how this identity is perpetuated. Situated on a remote Norwegian island in the arctic circle, it was built in 2008.[15] Known colloquially as the "doomsday vault," it stores seeds received from various seedbanks around the world, which are then made available in the case of emergencies caused by natural disasters, climate change, war or other factors. The vault thus safeguards the resources to regrow food for the planet, as well as to develop hybrid seeds that may be needed as the earth's growing conditions change. One of the major suppliers of seeds is the formerly Syria-based International Center for Agricultural Research in Dry Areas (ICARDA).

In 2012, the headquarters for ICARDA were moved from Aleppo to Lebanon due to the civil war in Syria. Because the workers had to evacuate rapidly, many seeds were left behind in the building. Syria thus became the first country to withdraw seeds from the seed vault (in effect, it withdrew its own backups, which it had stored there), to replenish the ICARDA archive and to grow food. The documentary moves between the sparse Norwegian island with its sleek storage vault; the office in the Bekaa Valley where ICARDA is now located, including the fields where seeds are being replanted, manipulated and harvested; and other spaces in Lebanon where landowners or refugees offer alternatives and insights into the ideology that undergirds the practices of the seed vault. *Wild Relatives* moves from the clinical interior of the seed vault, to observing young refugee women at work producing plants and hybrid seeds, to accompanying a refugee farmer, who is developing his own method of seed preservation through informal community-building. It focuses not on borders but rather on flows: seeds move from Lebanon to Norway and back again, and people move across borders within the Levant. *Wild Relatives* encourages us to visualize the flows that we cannot see: the geopolitical interests abetting the war in Syria and the neocolonial paternalism that lies beneath many attitudes of international organizations like the seed vault.

The voiceover in this film is, as in *A Magical Substance*, provided by Manna herself, but this time she speaks in Arabic, no longer reading the text of someone else (i.e., Lachmann) and delivering information in a tone that mirrors that of the disinterested voice of authority. Yet the narration offers a critical decolonial perspective on the film's images. For example, at one moment, it defines the "Green Revolution": "This movement, which brought agricultural production to an industrial scale believed it could end world hunger and, in the process, fight communism." The ostensibly altruistic motives of the capitalist West are thus immediately called into question via the explicit naming of Cold War geopolitical interests. The narration then goes on to link the Green Revolution to issues of labor and biodiversity, continuing, "This created major new problems, ushering in an era of farming without farmers. Modern seeds have steadily been eliminating local varieties," thus creating the pressing need to preserve seeds that are now on the brink of extinction: "This is why genebanks were created in the first place."

The genebank's location in the global north, in one of the world's wealthiest countries, whose affluence is rooted in resource extraction, directly implicates Norway in the causes of climate change and non-renewable resource dependence, which in large part make the seedbank necessary. The voiceover notes without significant inflection that the vault "has been dug into a mountain range where coal mining has been taking place for over a century." The seeds thus replace coal as the "resource" housed in the mountain. A scene captured in a static longshot is indicative of the film's subtle commentary on continuing neocolonial relations: in a Norwegian church, a family dedicates their infant. The priest gives the family a candle made by Norwegian nuns and a cloth, explaining, "that small cloth was made by women in Madagascar, symbolizing that she [the baby] is now part of the global Christian church."

The patronizing attitude of the Northerners toward the Arab seed producers is registered with a light hand by the camera in a scene documenting the partial replenishment of borrowed seeds in the vault. An official press opportunity shows the Arab ICARDA representative in conversation with a white Norwegian representative inside the vault. The latter says:

> You know, ideally, we have this as a security deposit for the world, and we hope, to be frank [looks meaningfully at the ICARDA rep] that it never needs to be used. Because *if things work around the world as they should* then we shouldn't need to take seeds out [italics mine].

It is unclear in this discursive moment if ICARDA and the SWANA countries whose seeds it collects are included in the "we" or whether they are "the world," that is, the beneficiaries of Norway's (and the global North's) foresight and planning. The tone is decidedly patronizing: Syria, *elsewhere*, is a place where things do not work as they *should*, and its nonfunctioning has no connection with what happens in the Global North, where things do work as they *ought to* and whom we can thank, ultimately, for the preservation of these seeds. When the ICARDA representative speaks to the incredible success of their efforts to replenish the withdrawn seeds, noting that, "normally, we plant in a normal year, 10,000 accessions. Last year we planted 33,000 between routine activities plus the 25,000 of Svalbard which is really a big achievement," the European representative responds, "It's a good thing you had the genebank CRP. You got money to do this!"

The film proceeds to highlight how the standardization of agriculture has diminished the wilder varieties of uncultivated seeds, many of which have become necessary for developing more resistant hybrids. As noted by the voiceover, ironically, the seedbank is now the only place where some of these wild seeds can be found. Thus, "development," that is, rationalization and innovation in agriculture, has both destroyed and preserved the seeds we may need more than ever in the near future. The film is full of these ironies. As previously mentioned, in another scene a Lebanese landowner discusses how it is more profitable to turn your land into a refugee camp than to grow food on it. He makes it clear that local agriculture is severely impacted by having to compete with imported produce. The same international structures of aid that make refugee camps more profitable than growing food are parallel to the organizations that develop resources like the international seedbank. The neocolonial politics of the situation are well-described by a phrase from Trinh Minh-ha's film *Reassemblage* (1983): "Create needs, then help." Absent a didactic tone or an overall affect of outrage or injustice, the film teases out the transnational economic interests that benefit from devastation (typically, in "other" places) and that work against sustainability in the interests of capital.

The film takes its title from the biological concept of wild relatives, "plant species that bear close resemblances to domesticated crops, but, being rougher around the edges, lack their taste, good looks, and consistency."[16] Yet despite their less desirable qualities, "because the wild relatives have survived with little or no help from people, they are hardy and persistent, and so can serve as lifelines when crops begin to fail."[17] This concept is never defined or even mentioned within the film itself, but it clearly shapes the way Manna positions many of her Arab subjects vis-à-vis the Global North. Like these wild seeds, the refugees we see planting, eating, working, smoking, dancing and generally thriving in the film have been left to their own devices and in the process proved resilient and resourceful: "Wild relatives, which have evolved to prioritize defense, often have layers of resistance to multiple threats."[18] The Arab as the wild relative of the European is a concept both explored and undermined throughout the film, which is full of counter-hegemonic images of Arabs: databank managers, women doing the detailed technical work of seed fertilization, a scientist in a headscarf describing the complex research she does at ICARDA. Manna's interest in women is again evident in this film. Women and girls are consistently represented throughout as central to the work of reproducing life through planting, growing and manipulating these life-saving seeds. Although men are present in the film, the camera seems drawn to the women who pile into the backs of vehicles, shuttle out to the fields and spend the day working the land, talking, eating and dancing during breaks, and sometimes smoking cigarettes (Figures 3.1 and 3.2). The women speak about their favorite dishes to eat or why they prefer working to being at home: "At home you can't say a word. Here I am with my friends." These

Figure 3.1 Manna's camera lingers on a wild relative at work in the fields.

Figure 3.2 Women heading to work in the fields for ICARDA in Lebanon.

friendships go back to Syria and represent the persistence of bonds across borders and through major upheavals.

As noted, care is taken not to represent development as a goal extrinsic or foreign to the Levant or to make scientific rationality the property of Europe and suggest a mystical, essential connection of Arabs to the land in lieu of sustainable progress. A cut from the seed vault at Svalbad to the orderly ICARDA fields in Lebanon suggests parallels in the rationalized industrial approach to agriculture between the two spaces. A representative at ICARDA explains double haploids to the audience, as well as how they represent innovations in achieving a "pure" plant variety. This is ironic given the film's celebration of hybridity: the mixing of peoples and approaches to the land that are seen in the film's mapping of the Bekaa Valley is, metaphorically speaking, an insistence on polyculture over the monocultures of the Green Revolution.

A 2021 *New Yorker* article suggests the West's dependency on the work of ICARDA. Because the spring season has become warmer, Hessian flies have begun to breed earlier in the year, allowing them to attack the wheat crops in Washington State at an earlier stage in their growth, which has devastated crops.[19] ICARDA works specifically with the wild relatives of domesticated strains of wheat in order to address issues such as insect infestations. Thus, American farmers may be dependent on their wild relatives (human and seed) from SWANA countries for crop survival going forward. *Wild Relatives'* depiction of women working on and with these seeds offers a different lens through which to read articles like the one in the *New Yorker*: the Arab woman, a silent, ignorant victim in the Western imaginary, works to rescue America from the effects of climate change caused by its own practices of overconsumption and waste (Figure 3.3).

Figure 3.3 A scientist at ICARDA explains haploids to the camera.

Crucially, it is through hybridization with other seeds that strains resistant to climate change can develop. Again, the film does not delve into this science, but the logic of the title reveals Manna's intention in this film, echoing the emphasis of films like *A Magical Substance* on hybridity as the future, on coexistence and mutual dependence as the way forward. It is the hybrids that will survive. Those that have persisted against all odds will create the conditions to live; seeds and people who have remained committed to notions of purity or ethnonational sovereignty may not be equipped to survive the challenges that war, occupation and climate change bring.

If the film has a heart, it is located in the portrait of Walid El-Youssef, a refugee from the outskirts of Aleppo, now organically farming in the Bekaa Valley (Figure 3.4). He describes how his father taught him farming from a young age. El-Youssef has started his own DIY community seedbank: "We collect seeds whenever we find people planting local varieties. We try to keep in touch and build strong friendships. We exchange seeds, as well as experiences and ideas with one another." This community seedbank enacts in practice what Guha's argues: "in the absence of social regeneration environmental regeneration has very little chance of succeeding."[20] Questions of equity and social justice cannot be separated from ecological concerns in a decolonial framework. The farmer summarizes that the work he does is "for the earth and for us." A close-up of worms in El-Youssef's compost provides a rich visual contrast with the sterility of previous images in the film. The moist earth replete with worms suggests the organic reproduction of life and the regeneration of soil and of culture. El-Youssef notes that the value of the worm to the soil is universal and exclaims, "This is the richest compost in the world here.

Figure 3.4 Walid El-Youssef in *Wild Relatives* (2018).

It cannot be valued in money." This wild relative offers a decolonial alternative to farming rooted in industrial models and dependent on neocolonial paternalistic practices of aid. This countermodel does not posit that humans need to disappear for renewal to occur but rather offers the patient (re)building of human relationships with each other and with the land as an image of hope in the doomsday gloom.

Biocolonization and Refusal in *Foragers* (2022)

Foragers differs from Manna's other documentary features in its use of scripted scenes to stage encounters between Palestinians and representatives of the Israeli state. Foraging greens, such as za'atar and 'akkoub, is outlawed by the Israeli government.[21] The Israeli Nature and Parks Authority (operating under the military) hunts and fines pickers. The film situates the criminalization of foraging within the larger Israeli project of dispossessing Palestinians of their ancestral land rights and targeting the fabric of Palestinian cultural life, as these greens are central to the seasonal Palestinian diet. *Foragers* makes clear that the prohibition on picking is also good business: Israeli Jews commercially farm these greens for profit. By clamping down on foraging practices, the state creates a captive market for the herbs. Moving between scenes of the accused being questioned in the Israeli legal system, of people foraging and being fined, and vignettes of Manna's own parents foraging, relaxing and spending time with extended family, the film discursively and visually counters dominant Israeli narratives. Challenging the discursive hegemony of the occupying regime, *Foragers* explores how the land itself—the very herbs and plants that grow from the ground—is occupied through biocolonial practices of appropriating wild seeds for commercial farming and monopolizing their sale while banning wild harvesting. The film foregrounds a sense of Palestinian cultural identity rooted not in a nationalist teleology but rather in knowledge systems and practices connected to the land and its native inhabitants.

The Israeli state claims that its ban on foraging is rooted in sustainability because these greens are in danger of extinction. *Foragers* challenges the colonialist ecological argument by situating harvesting and consumption within larger Israeli policies of agricultural commercialization, control of access to space and the active attrition of Palestinian lands. Paraphrasing Guha's discussion of a "Third World" ecological perspective, Manna offers a decolonial perspective where issues of food production and sustainability "deeply involve questions of equity as well as economic and political redistribution."[22] The purported extinction of a plant, in this framework, cannot be separated from the way it has been regulated and commercialized by the occupying culture, nor can it be analyzed in separation from the human communities that rely on it.[23] In his writing on African ecocriticism, Anthony Vital argues that "a consideration of the role [] various discourses of nature play in a region's social processes would enable focus on the flows of power that give ecology its social value."[24] Applying this to Manna's own non-Western decolonial ecocritical approach, I emphasize here the discursive struggle the film wages against Israeli narratives of legitimate land use. It resists representations of nature that isolate it from the social, political and economic histories that shape it.

An environmental approach is crucial for understanding the ways in which the Palestinian economy and agriculture have been decimated by Israeli tactics. Separation walls in the Occupied Palestinian Territories (OPT) not only separate farmers from their land, they are, in many cases, built on confiscated fertile land, now unfarmable because the Israeli Army has "declared the buffer zone [around the wall] a 'closed military area.'"[25] The Israeli state controls the water supplies needed to irrigate fields and has annexed large areas of green space in the occupied West Bank for illegal settlements.[26] Many Palestinians see settlements as the real cause of the reduction in wild 'akkoub:

> If Israel were serious about conservation, [Chef Fadi] Kattan says, it would leave Palestinians to pick and grow Akoub the way they have for generations and focus instead on stopping the expansion of Jewish settlements. "The largest environmental threat is called the settlements. Har Homa, which is opposite to us, used to be a forest," Kattan says. "Now it's a forest of white buildings."[27]

Caroline Abu-Sada observes that "increased Israeli control over Palestinian agriculture has received very little attention from human rights organizations and in the scholarly literature on the Israeli occupation."[28] *Foragers* addresses these gaps via a different medium, while contributing to the work of ethnographies that "follow food," as a method of tracing the economic, environmental, political and social relations that are bound up with food's production and consumption.[29] Manna's film follows the greens from field to table, including their regulation and "illegal" sale on the streets.

Without drawing a literal map, *Foragers* enacts a form of countermapping, showing how within the occupied territory various "borders" are drawn, while also undermining them by documenting Palestinian resistance, persistence in the land (*sumud*) and outright refusal of the settler colonial administration, creating an alternative imaging of the region centered on Palestinian ingredients. The film's emphasis on scenes of testimony is central to this political topography: mapping itself is a practice of discursive power. For example, a countermap might use original indigenous place-names as opposed to those imposed by the colonizer in order to make visible the way in which histories of colonization mark the land.[30] As a practice that can also make visible concealed "current carceral configurations," countermapping in *Foragers* reveals Israeli reterritorializing of the commons as a field of surveillance and criminal activity.[31] The opening shot evokes this through its combination of drone footage with a sparse electronic soundtrack (Figure 3.5).

The image of the land, shot from a disembodied aerial perspective, is paired with music that connotes an alien presence and alienating perspective on what is seen. This militarized view from above produces the land's long-time inhabitants as targets, criminals or threats to the land. This is a way of seeing imbued with violence, which the soundtrack emphasizes is an invasive and foreign framework.[32] The opening shot contrasts starkly with the

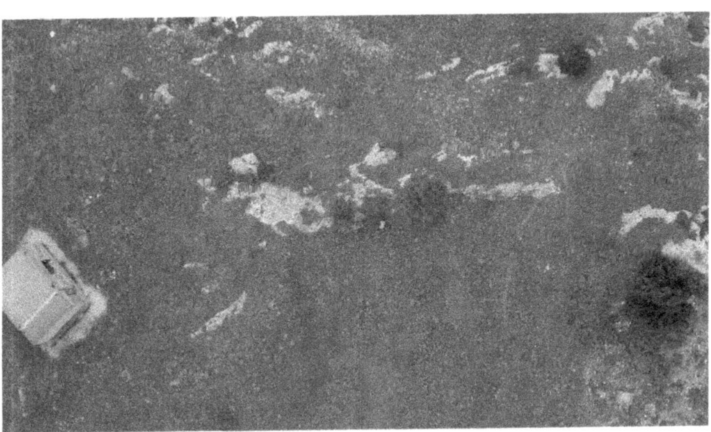

Figure 3.5 Opening drone footage produces the landscape as an area of risk.

following embodied POV shots that put us into the perspective of a forager. The drone shot cuts to a forager smoking in his car. Now *he* watches the enforcement agents without being seen. When the agents go into the field to "hunt" foragers, he slashes their tires. Thus, the more embodied, handheld camerawork rooted on the ground or in the land puts us not only into a forager's POV but also a forager with whose act of guerilla resistance the camera encourages us to sympathize. Much time throughout the film is reserved for images of the landscape and vegetation both with and without Palestinians present. These images are a visual rejoinder to the notion that Palestine naturally lacks fertility, and it slowly invites us to see the landscape through Palestinian eyes. From this perspective, the expanses of the green we see before us are rich with nourishment and sources of sustenance. Only someone with no relationship to the land would see this place as empty or infertile, the film affirms. By contrast, when Israelis are in the landscape, they are presented as a disturbance or intrusion. For example, in one scene they off-road in a jeep through a landscape in which Aziza, Manna's mother, precariously sits. She is almost camouflaged in the grass, communing with the plants around her (see Figure 3.7).

One of the many discursive successes of the Israeli state has been propagating the narrative that Palestine was just a "pile of rocks" before Israeli settlers came and "made the desert bloom."[33] Characterizations of underdevelopment or the natives as unable to properly utilize the natural resources at their disposal echo throughout the histories of colonialism. Processes of biocolonization are "seen as justifiable and as justified because [existing inhabitants] are regarded as *sine scientia*, without science, and, therefore, without genuine knowledge of the natural world."[34] I want to take a moment to elaborate on biocolonization here because it is central to understanding the decolonial discursive struggle that *Foragers* wages against Israeli policies. In her book *Science, Colonialism, and Indigenous Peoples*, Laurelyn Whitt defines biocolonialism as using "force or coercion (economic or otherwise)" that "involves or facilitates the removal, processing, conversion into private property, and commodification of indigenous genetic resources by agents of the dominant culture(s)."[35] Whitt offers a list of possible results of biocolonialism, most of which describe well the impact of Israeli commercial farming of *'akkoub and za'atar* and the concomitant ban on foraging. For example, possible results of biocolonialism include the "creation of new, or the exacerbation of existing, internal or external political struggles"; the "disruption or discrediting of indigenous knowledge and value systems"; the "imposition of concepts, practices, and values that further the economic and political interests of the dominant culture"; and a "loss of political and economic autonomy and increased dependency on the dominant culture(s)."[36] While biocolonization as a subset of neocolonial practices was highlighted in *Wild Relatives*, in *Foragers* it is an active component of the settler colonial practices of the Israeli state.

Foragers excerpts a 1978 interview with early Israeli za'atar growers that originally aired on Israel Channel 1. The interviewer laughs while noting that by selling the Arabs za'atar, they are basically "sell[ing] ice to the Eskimos [*sic*]". She admires the way these entrepreneuring za'atar manufacturers have "combined the advantages of the land of Israel and the Jewish mind." The interviewees (Ze'ev and Yoram Ben Harut) explain that "The nature authorities had to instruct customs to confiscate all za'atar but ours" so that only Israeli za'atar can be exported to Jordan, highlighting the ways in which border control is used to benefit the Israeli economy while making most agricultural endeavors unsustainable for Palestinians. The interviewer summarizes to the younger Ben Harut: "for your father, za'atar is Zionism. Za'atar is coexistence." The son concludes that "Za'atar is Israel." Within the course of a short interview, the avowed "national food of the Arabs" is identified with and shown to be controlled by Israeli producers and is then definitionally linked to Zionism and "coexistence" (the form that coexistence takes here is clear from the instructions the customs officers have received). Finally, za'atar *is* Israel, and the discursive domination is complete, supported by state power and disseminated via the mainstream media.

The film's interview with the head of a Kibbutz farm (Nabil Ni'coula) is central to its dismantling of the argument that conservation is the primary motivator for the ban on foraging. Manna's offscreen voice interviews Ni'coula, reversing the pattern the film has established previously where suspected foragers, visible onscreen, are interrogated by an offscreen voice representing Israeli legal and judicial authority. Also, in contrast to these earlier scenes, the interview with the head of the 'akkoub farm is unscripted. As Manna's questions become increasingly pressing, Ni'coula grows visibly uncomfortable, shifting around, looking off camera and saying, "that's enough." He explains that all of the 'akkoub is sold to the Arab sector, and Manna inquires as to why they began cultivating it. He responds immediately, "Business. It makes good money." After a pause, he supplements, "And because it's going extinct in the wild. To make it available and take care of nature." Business is clearly first, with the more publicity-friendly language of sustainability providing further justification.

The interview is rich in its struggle for definitional power over the farming and picking of 'akkoub, so I quote it at length here:

Manna: Are there any Arabs that plant ['akkoub] or is it only Jews?
Ni'coula: No Arabs. They tried and failed.
Manna: Why does it succeed only with Jews?
Ni'coula: [Turns away from the camera.] The climate plays a role. And Arabs don't have land insurance. If there's a crop failure, it's a total loss. Here in the kibbutz, they're insured. Floods, whatever . . . they're covered

Manna: Who covers?
Ni'coula: The insurance. All the kibbutzes are insured.
Manna: So good or bad crop, they're fine.
Ni'coula: Yes, if the failure is due to weather, they get reimbursed.
Manna: They've made life easy for themselves.
Ni'coula: [smiles] Totally.
Manna: Why don't the Arabs insure their land?
Ni'coula: Because they don't have large *dunams* of land. They can't really afford insurance. Insurance is very expensive. *'Akkoub and za'atar* are banned, because Arabs like them very much. They are afraid of it going extinct. . . . When it's pulled from its root.
Manna: But *we* don't pull it out from its roots. [Italics mine]
Ni'coula: Some do with a spade, or pick the plants too young.
Manna: Out of fear! To escape the patrol. Right? Historically no one takes the roots.
Ni'coula: That's true.
Manna: So where is the risk?
Ni'coula: The risk . . . [walks off camera, but the camera follows]. Don't make me talk more.

Manna positions cultural and historically rooted practices of food gathering against less sustainable agricultural practices (the farms survive because they are insured against the climate) that are rooted in profit. Ni'coula knows that Arabs are a captive market and that Israeli policies have increased unsustainable foraging practices by criminalizing the activity. The interview is notable for the point at which Manna's questioning voice insists on her own identity within these discursive struggles, "*We* don't pick the roots," she says, including herself in the group of Palestinians in question. This identification is further developed in the film through the recurrence of her parents as characters. In this interview Manna engages in an on-the-ground struggle against Israeli discourse, putting her in solidarity with her characters who stage multiple forms of resistance to the law in the film's many legal scenes.

Foragers presents five encounters between accused foragers and Israeli legal officials. The voice of authority, which questions, is always offscreen and disembodied. The use of different offscreen voices in these scenes suggests that the law operates structurally and systemically, independent of the individuals occupying the official position. The violent generality of the law is unconcerned with individual Palestinians' long-standing relationships to the land where they forage or whether there are nine mouths to feed at home while the Israeli state enforces conditions of abject poverty. It is not a law meant to benefit or protect the Palestinians who stand before it. The law, on the side of the colonizer, positions itself as rational (foraging is a problem of sustainability, therefore. . .) against its Arab other. But the various discursive strategies employed by the accused are methods of speaking back to, frustrating and refusing to acknowledge the absolute power of the colonial state over Palestinians. The defendants are shown in medium shot or medium close-up in front of the camera, either in the courthouse or outside of it (Figure 3.6). They speak not only to the legal authority but also to us, as spectators, who bear witness. It is tempting to compare this staging to *Rashomon's* iconic courtroom scenes, but the intent and effect here couldn't be more different. This is not a meditation on the relativity of truth in the wake of a loss of faith in humanity. This is about the violence, disingenuousness and irrationality of a colonial law and the resistant speech of the occupied.

The first accused, Ahmad Hosni (a character played by an actor), denies he has picked za'atar since he has plenty at home. But he couches this within a longer dialogue that does not conform to the modes of speech required and expected by the law. When asked if he picked the herb, he responds, "Let me tell you something. I am part of nature. Nature is . . . me. When I go to nature, I go in order to find myself." Later, he insists, "I won't answer you. I'll tell you again. I am nature, OK? I would not harm myself." The law positions the accused as separate from and acting on nature, as posing a threat to it, but Hosni refuses this framework, seeing himself as inseparable from what is called nature. This gestures back to the discussion of *Wild Relatives*, whereby a decolonial understanding of nature renders it inseparable from humans and social relationships. Hosni's attempt to expand or reframe the terms of interrogation, before a law that only understands the human as acting on a nature external to itself, is a form of decolonial resistance. The film supports this alternative knowledge system, depicting the activities of the pickers as part of a natural annual cycle. For example, one enforcement officer says to another,

Figure 3.6 One of the accused challenges the logic of the settler colonial state.

"There's a family that always comes here around this time," as if the Palestinian foragers were part of the local wild life. He continues, "They come to the areas of Karmiel, and Qaditha" as though he were passing on knowledge of the migratory patterns of local fauna. When the judge inquires, "Do you know that it's illegal to pick za'atar?" Hosni replies, "That I know. For Arabs it's definitely forbidden. For Jews it's always ok." He responds with his knowledge, not only of the law but of its discriminatory application. Hosni pierces through the veneer of a rational and objective law to define its true intent as targeting Palestinian self-sustenance and criminalizing their cultural practices. To again reference Laurelyn Whitt: indigenous "resistance to bio-colonialism . . . demonstrates how the law's own rhetoric of neutrality acts as an ideological cloaking device."[37]

Another accused (Nadia Na'amneh, listed as playing herself) challenges not the facticity of her picking but rather the application of the law. Countering the "rationality" of the law, she offers an alternative logic for the persecuted. She rhetorically interrogates the state, demanding, "Why do you wait for me the entire day, until I'm exhausted, then confiscate [the greens] and humiliate me and tell me it's forbidden? Why don't you stop me the minute you see me picking?" Her speech directly challenges discourses of conservation as motivating the law against foraging (why are they letting her pick all day before approaching her if these are endangered plants?). Instead, humiliation and the consumption of Palestinian energy and time in fruitless endeavors are the true effects of the law's application. Nadia pokes another hole into the state's avowed concern for sustainability when she states, "They just want us to buy it instead."

Many of the accused insist that what they've picked is for household use only. Although the off-camera voice declares that this isn't a legally relevant distinction, or that the amount they've harvested is far too much for a single household, these subjects refuse the logic of the state, insisting again on their own logic—foraging food to feed their family is not a criminal activity. This rejection of colonial juridical discourse asserts Palestinian sovereignty, despite the subjugated position of the accused.[38] One defendant adds to her claim of picking only for home use, offering a historical *and* environmental argument:

> We have been foraging from this land all our lives. Since the age of my father and grandfather. My father used to bring back stems this long [spreads out her arms to show a long section]. . . . Since you banned us, za'atar is harder to find. We don't find what we used to.

She takes a moment to educate the authorities, "Za'atar needs to be trimmed, like all plants. The more it's clipped, the stronger it grows back." This lecture forms a backdrop to the later interview with the 'akkoub farm head, Ni'coula, who claims Palestinian foraging practices are endangering the plants. The viewer has already taken in Palestinian knowledge of the relationship between foraging and plant propagation in the wild; thus, the rehearsed arguments of Ni'coula ring hollow.

The last of the interrogation scenes is given to Samir Na'amneh, listed in the credits as playing himself (and presumably of some relation to Nadia, above). His position is one of outright refusal. He does not acknowledge the legitimacy of the Israeli state and its laws, nor does he deny his actions: "I am waiting for this to be over so I can go back to foraging 'akkoub," he tells the state's proxy. He insists, "Do whatever you want. I won't pay a penny. I won't justify your law." Samir questions the very legality of the law itself as imposed by an occupying administration, asking rhetorically of his interrogator, "What protected species? This land isn't yours! Neither is the plant!" He connects his refusal with the futurity of his people and the Palestinian politics of *sumud*, or steadfastness in the land, as he promises, "I'll also be caught in 2050 with my children and grandchildren." The magistrate vents, "I can't talk any sense into you," but the various scenes of legal inquisition have revealed that the *sense* of the colonial law is open to contestation. Hoda El Shakry frames *sumud* as a form of infrapolitics that reflect hope and futurity, as is evident here in Samir's promise/threat.[39] Eric Ritskes argues that "When one has been forgotten, relegated to the zone of non-being and perpetual death, the only action left besides waiting for death, is *refusal*."[40] For Ritskes, "refusal is a fugitive move that generatively builds a new, alternative future within the land."[41]

As a figure deeply associated with the refusal to recognize an unjust law, it is perhaps unsurprising that Sophocles' *Antigone* was the first play to be staged by students of Drama Academy Ramallah, the first theater school for Palestinians in the West Bank.[42] This classical icon of grief and mourning, who speaks truth to power, certainly resonates with the Palestinian context, and the Palestinians represented in *Foragers* enact an equally inspiring "politics of counter-sovereignty."[43] Coming from a place of much less privilege than Antigone, and suffering *decades* of loss, death, humiliations and displacement at the hands of the state, the characters in *Foragers* continue to refuse the arbitrary and unjust abuse of state power. Paraphrasing Bonnie Honig on Antigone, the accused here "act[] politically in conditions of impossibility."[44] Like Creon, the Israeli state sees as its right "the quest to own the power of definition."[45] By staging these interrogations for the camera, the film "solicits publics" over and above the interrogators, and, after Bhabha, through these scenes "other 'denied' knowledges enter upon the dominant discourse and estrange the basis of its authority—its rules of recognition."[46]

At one point, the film's aspect ratio shifts to include cellphone footage shot by a forager in the process of being fined (Kayed Boshnaq, 2020). This footage provides a cinema verité perspective contrasting with the staging of the other scenes. It also puts the officers, rather than the accused, in front of the camera, while still centering the accused's voice. Boshnaq negotiates his position of relative powerless by documenting the state's actions and resisting through his speech. One of the officers asks him to turn off his phone, but he does not. "The season of fines has begun," he declares, naming the amount of the standard fine and thus giving the incident an almost ritual cyclical dimension while also making clear that fines have not deterred the resilient Palestinians. Boshnaq declares, "May they use this to buy medicine for all their children. Do you see him?. . . Medicine for all their children. What a nation of. . . . Viva, Viva, Palestina!" Like Samir, Boshnaq refuses and persists. He also uses language to indicate the irony and fundamental inequity of the situation. The Israeli state does not need the money, while many of the Palestinians they take it from require international humanitarian aid, with their own children often denied medical care due to checkpoint closures and delays or the destruction of infrastructure.

Manna's parents appear in *Foragers* as central to the sequence of images, and her mother Aziza, in particular, is repeatedly framed in nature, connecting her with the landscape (Figure 3.7). Scenes of the Manna's foraging, going to the lake and preparing greens at home work to situate the filmmaker in relation to the heritage of the land and a Palestinian way of knowing this environment. In one scene, her parents picnic by a body of water, commenting on the fauna and reminiscing about past times spent there. Aziza enters the water and swims, at home in nature. Later, at night, this image contrasts with the lights of a patrol car seen on the far side of the water, a CB radio sounding incessantly. Visually and sonically, the film makes clear who intrudes upon the land.

Eventually, Aziza is connected with a figure who has recurred throughout the film: Zeidan lives in a situation that seems relatively impoverished. His living quarters are in ruins in the middle of a former village. He sleeps

Figure 3.7 Aziza Manna in the grass.

Figure 3.8 Zeidan with Kushkou.

under the stars with his pack of dogs and forages for subsistence. We see him being fined and harassed, returning at night to gather the ‘akkoub that the authorities have dumped from his bag. He spends time with his dogs in the fields and goes to town to buy them food. Moreso than even Aziza, Zeidan is represented as part of the landscape, as much an animal inhabitant as the dogs that sleep and forage with him (Figure 3.8). Aziza visits the extended family to enjoy a meal and some conversation and is sent to Zeidan's home to pick up some ‘akkoub. The film ends on this scene, which deepens and affirms the Palestinian relationship with the land. In an extreme long shot we see the women approaching the ruins in which Zeidan lives. They reminisce about who lived where on this patch of land, with Aziza noting the (former) location of her family home (Figure 3.9). This recurring location, then, is finally revealed to have ancestral significance for Manna herself and links the forced expulsion of Palestinians from their land to the criminalization of Palestinian foraging practices.

Foragers, like its subjects, refuses the state-enforced separation of the Palestinian from the land in the name of sustainability. It challenges the monopoly that the Israeli state claims on making sense, voicing competing discourses and ways of knowing. Challenging the biocolonial premises of the ban on foraging, it enacts, after Greg Burris an emancipatory politics that “indicates the power of refusal, the ability to say no and thereby to clear a path for the introduction of new possibilities.”[47] We will see in the following chapter that environmental politics are also present in the films of Larissa Sansour (with Søren Lind) in, although Sansour's engagement with the future is staged in more artificial settings.

Figure 3.9 The final scene of *Foragers* (2022).

Notes

1 Some other examples of creative Palestinian forms of countermapping include Annelys de Vet, ed., *Subjective Atlas of Palestine* (Rotterdam: 010 Publishers, 2007); and the virtual collages and images of Palestinian territory circulated online by young Palestinians in refugee camps, discussed in Leila Khalili, "Virtual Nation: Palestinian Cyberculture in Lebanese Camps," in *Palestine, Israel, and the Politics of Popular Culture*, ed. Rebecca L. Stein and Ted Swedenburg (Durham: Duke University Press, 2005).

2 Alexander Sager, "Mapping and Countermapping Shifting Borders," *European Journal of Political Theory* 2, no. 3 (2022): 602.

3 Sager, "Mapping," 602.

4 Sebastian Cobarrubias, "Countermapping," in *Encyclopedia of Human Geography*, ed. Barney Warf (Thousand Oaks: Sage Publications, 2010), 596.

5 Nick Gill et al., "Carceral Circuitry: New Directions in Carceral Geography," *Progress in Human Geography* 42, no. 2 (2018): 186.

6 Gill et al., "Carceral Circuitry," 188.

7 Interestingly, given the connections in Manna's work with Norway, the term deep ecology was coined by Norwegian philosopher Arne Naess. See Ramachandra Guha, "Radical American Environmentalism and Wilderness Preservation: A Third World Critique," *Environmental Ethics* 11, no. 1 (1989): 72.

8 Cara Cilano and Elizabeth DeLoughrey, "Against Authenticity: Global Knowledges and Postcolonial Ecocriticism," *Interdisciplinary Studies in Literature and Environment* 14, no. 1 (Winter 2007): 71.

9 Cilano and DeLoughrey, "Against Authenticity," 71.
10 Cilano and DeLoughrey, 79.
11 John Collins, *Global Palestine* (New York: Columbia University Press, 2011), 117.
12 Collins, *Global Palestine*, 117.
13 Graham Huggan and Helen Tiffin, *Postcolonial Ecocriticism: Literature, Animals, Environment* (London; New York: Routledge, 2015), 19.
14 Manna's "Government Quarter Study" (2017) was a replica of three pillars of the government building in Oslo, the site of a domestic terrorist attack in 2011 by Anders Behring Breivik, a far-right Norwegian who was trying to save Norway (and Western Europe) from a Muslim takeover.
15 The site's construction was funded by the Norwegian government, and is maintained by Norway in conjunction with transnational NGO's.
16 Helen Sullivan, "A Syrian Seed Bank's Fight to Survive," *The New Yorker*, October 19, 2021, accessed August 1, 2023, www.newyorker.com/news/annals-of-a-warming-planet/a-syrian-seed-banks-fight-to-survive.
17 Sullivan, "A Syrian Seed Bank's Fight."
18 Sullivan.
19 Sullivan.
20 Guha, "Radical American," 81–82.
21 Za'atar (also known as Wild Hyssop) is the herb that also gives its name to the spice mix. 'Akkoub is a thorny plant to which Palestinians attribute a variety of health benefits, something made clear in the film.
22 Guha, 81.
23 Nor can it be separated from Israeli infrastructure projects, particularly around the illegal settlements and the construction of the apartheid wall, which also have a detrimental effect on the ecosystem.
24 Anthony Vital, "Toward an African Ecocriticism: Postcolonialism, Ecology and 'Life & Times of Michael K,'" *Research in African Literatures* 39, no. 1 (Spring 2008): 90.
25 Caroline Abu-Sada, "Cultivating Dependence: Palestinian Agriculture Under the Israeli Occupation," in *The Power of Inclusive Exclusion: Anatomy of Israeli Rule in the Occupied Palestinian Territories*, ed. Adi Ophir, Michal Givoni, and Sari Hanafi (New York: Zone Books, 2009), 429. Appendix 1 has a useful overview of the difficulties farmers have accessing and cultivating their land due to the wall and to the weaponization of checkpoints and permit bureaucracy.
26 "The Staggering Economic Cost of Occupation: The Palestinian Economy Would be at Least Twice as Large without Israeli Occupation, UNCTAD Report Says," *United Nations Conference on Trade and Development*, September 6, 2016, accessed August 1, 2023, https://unctad.org/news/staggering-economic-cost-occupation-palestinian-economy-would-be-least-twice-large-without; "Economic Restrictions in the West Bank exact $50 Billion Toll between 2000 and 2020," *United Nations Conference on Trade and Development*, November 22, 2022, accessed August 1, 2023, https://unctad.org/news/economic-restrictions-west-bank-exact-50-billion-toll-between-2000-and-2020; "Responsibility for Killing 14-Year-Old

Palestinian Lies Primarily with Commanders Who Ordered Armed Ambush," *B'Tselem*, March 26, 2014, accessed August 1, 2023, www.btselem.org/firearms/20140326_killing_of_yusef_a_shawamreh_deir_al_asal; "Propagation of Gundelia Declines in Salfit Due to Settlement," *The Palestinian Information Center*, March 8, 2018, accessed August 1, 2023, https://english.palinfo.com/news/2018/3/8/Propagation-of-Gundelia-declines-in-Salfit-due-to-settlement.

27 Eliyahu Kamisher, "The Fight for a Flower," *Roads & Kingdoms*, April 23, 2018, accessed August 1, 2023, https://roadsandkingdoms.com/2018/the-fight-for-a-flower/; see also, for example, "Propagation of Gundelia."

28 Abu-Sada, "Cultivating Dependence," 418.

29 Ian Cook et al., "Geographies of Food: Following," *Progress in Human Geography* 30, no. 5 (2006).

30 This example is particularly germane for Palestinians, who understand the power of insisting on the older Arabic names for places, which have been violently replaced by Hebrew nomenclature.

31 Gill et al., "Carceral Circuitry," 193.

32 See also my discussion of Basma Alsharif's films in terms of the use of drone technology in Chapter 5.

33 This is a baseline for forms of biolcolonization as articulated by Laurelyn Whitt, *Science, Colonialism, and Indigenous Peoples: The Cultural Politics of Law and Knowledge* (Cambridge: Cambridge University Press, 2009).

34 Whitt, *Science*, 27.

35 Whitt, 23.

36 Whitt, 23–24.

37 Whitt, 28.

38 See Steven Salaita, *Inter/Nationalism: Decolonizing Native America and Palestine* (Minneapolis: University of Minnesota Press, 2016), 159.

39 Hoda El Shakry, "Palestine and the Aesthetics of the Future Impossible," *Interventions: International Journal of Postcolonial Studies* 23, no. 5 (2021).

40 Eric Ritskes, "Beyond and Against White Settler Colonialism in Palestine: Fugitive Futurities in Amir Nizar Zuabi's 'The Underground Ghetto City of Gaza,'" *Cultural Studies Critical Methodologies* 17, no. 1 (2017): 81.

41 Ritskes, "Beyond and Against," 81.

42 Bonnie Honig, *Antigone Interrupted* (Cambridge: Cambridge University Press, 2013), 10; Yonith Benhamou and Lorenzo Kamel, "Setting the Stage," *The Jerusalem Post*, February 17, 2010, accessed August 1, 2023, www.jpost.com/arts-and-culture/books/setting-the-stage.

43 Honig, *Antigone*, 10.

44 Honig, 8.

45 Honig, 140.

46 Homi K. Bhabha, *The Location of Culture* (London; New York: Routledge, 1994), 162.

47 Greg Burris, *The Palestinian Idea: Film, Media, and the Radical Imagination* (Philadelphia: Temple University Press, 2019), 54–55.

Bibliography

Abu-Sada, Caroline. "Cultivating Dependence: Palestinian agriculture under the Israeli occupation." In *The Power of Inclusive Exclusion: Anatomy of Israeli rule in the occupied Palestinian territories*, edited by Adi Ophir, Michal Givoni, and Sari Hanafi, 413–33. New York: Zone Books, 2009.

Benhamou, Yonith, and Lorenzo Kamel. "Setting the Stage." *The Jerusalem Post*, February 17, 2010. www.jpost.com/arts-and-culture/books/setting-the-stage.

Bhabha, Homi K. *The Location of Culture*. London; New York: Routledge, 1994.

Burris, Greg. *The Palestinian Idea: Film, Media, and the Radical Imagination*. Philadelphia: Temple University Press, 2019.

Cilano, Cara, and Elizabeth DeLoughrey. "Against Authenticity: Global Knowledges and Postcolonial Ecocriticism." *Interdisciplinary Studies in Literature and Environment* 14, no. 1 (Winter 2007): 71–87.

Cobarrubias, Sebastian. "Countermapping." In *Encyclopedia of Human Geography*, edited by Barney Warf, 596. Thousand Oaks: Sage Publications, 2010.

Collins, John. *Global Palestine*. New York: Columbia University Press, 2011.

Cook, Ian et al. "Geographies of Food: Following." *Progress in Human Geography* 30, no. 5 (2006): 655–66.

"Economic Restrictions in the West Bank exact $50 Billion Toll between 2000 and 2020." *United Nations Conference on Trade and Development*, November 22, 2022. Accessed August 1, 2023. https://unctad.org/news/economic-restrictions-west-bank-exact-50-billion-toll-between-2000-and-2020.

El Shakry, Hoda. "Palestine and the Aesthetics of the Future Impossible." *Interventions: International Journal of Postcolonial Studies* 23, no. 5 (2021): 669–90.

Gill, Nick et al. "Carceral Circuitry: New directions in carceral geography." *Progress in Human Geography* 42, no. 2 (2018): 183–204.

Guha, Ramachandra. "Radical American Environmentalism and Wilderness Preservation: A Third World Critique." *Environmental Ethics* 11, no. 1 (1989): 71–83.

Honig, Bonnie. *Antigone Interrupted*. Cambridge: Cambridge University Press, 2013.

Huggan, Graham, and Helen Tiffin. *Postcolonial Ecocriticism: Literature, Animals, Environment*. London; New York: Routledge, 2015.

Kamisher, Eliyahu. "The Fight for a Flower." *Roads & Kingdoms*, April 23, 2018. https://roadsandkingdoms.com/2018/the-fight-for-a-flower/.

"Propagation of Gundelia Declines in Salfit due to Settlement." *The Palestinian Information Center*, March 8, 2018. Accessed August 1, 2023. https://english.palinfo.com/news/2018/3/8/Propagation-of-Gundelia-declines-in-Salfit-due-to-settlement.

"Responsibility for Killing 14-Year-Old Palestinian Lies Primarily with Commanders Who Ordered Armed Ambush." *B'Tselem*, March 26, 2014. www.btselem.org/firearms/20140326_killing_of_yusef_a_shawamreh_deir_al_asal.

Ritskes, Eric. "Beyond and Against White Settler Colonialism in Palestine: Fugitive Futurities in Amir Nizar Zuabi's 'The Underground Ghetto City of Gaza.'" *Cultural Studies Critical Methodologies* 17, no. 1 (2017): 78–86.

Sager, Alexander. "Mapping and Countermapping Shifting Borders." *European Journal of Political Theory* 2, no. 3 (2022): 601–7.

Salaita, Steven. *Inter/Nationalism: Decolonizing Native America and Palestine*. Minneapolis: University of Minnesota Press, 2016.

"The Staggering Economic Cost of Occupation: The Palestinian Economy would be at Least Twice as Large without Israeli Occupation, UNCTAD Report Says." *United Nations Conference on Trade and Development*, September 6, 2016. https://unctad.org/news/staggering-economic-cost-occupation-palestinian-economy-would-be-least-twice-large-without.

Sullivan, Helen. "A Syrian Seed Bank's Fight to Survive." *The New Yorker*, October 19, 2021. www.newyorker.com/news/annals-of-a-warming-planet/a-syrian-seed-banks-fight-to-survive.

Vet, Annelys de, ed. *Subjective Atlas of Palestine*. Rotterdam: 010 Publishers, 2007.

Vital, Anthony. "Toward an African Ecocriticism: Postcolonialism, Ecology and 'Life & Times of Michael K.'" *Research in African Literatures* 39, no. 1 (Spring 2008): 87–106.

Whitt, Laurelyn. *Science, Colonialism, and Indigenous Peoples: The Cultural Politics of Law and Knowledge*. Cambridge: Cambridge University Press, 2009.

4 In the Future Palestine Was . . .

Larissa Sansour's Dystopian futurisms

Palestinian futurisms

In their own singular ways, each of the filmmakers discussed in this book are constructing Palestinian futurisms, but the futurist moniker most obviously applies to Larissa Sansour's speculative visions. Lital Levy argues that Sansour's "dystopic futurism offers the most radical temporal revisioning of recent Palestinian cultural production."[1] She observes, "A kind of quite *sumud* in her cinematic rendering of Palestinian time, but it is irreducible to the temporality of waiting or return."[2] Her work does not invoke a future premised on a revolutionary progress narrative or the linear horizon of return but a restaging of the present in an elsewhere/elsewhen to generate alternate potentialities. Gil Hochberg emphasizes the postnational nature of films like *In the Future They Ate from the Finest Porcelain* (2016), which espouse "nonutopian, nonnationalist, nonnostalgic hope,"[3] and look to the future as "the time of imagining Palestine."[4] Nayrouz Abu Hatoum reinforces the films' postnationalism, noting that "While Sansour's work might hint at some attachment to statehood, it is done through sarcasm in which the future state is laughable or dysfunctional, spatially and politically."[5] What seems particularly powerful about Sansour's work is that it works through grief and loss, at the same time playing out impossible alternatives to the present tinged with absurdity or critique, and yet all the while creating a space of imaginative engagement that enables perspectival shifts and the emergence of new lines of flight out of present impasses. Hoda El Shakry discusses Sansour's trilogy (*A Space Exodus* [2009], *Nation Estate* [2012], and *In the Future They Ate from the Finest Porcelain*) alongside other Palestinian works that she argues "ultimately illustrate the critical potential of impossible acts of imagination."[6] Sansour's films stage "unfulfillable Palestinian futures," but this makes them no less radical as creative acts of decolonial resistance.[7]

Unlike Manna's documentary practice, or Alsharif's more formally experimental audiovisual work, Larissa Sansour's films (since *A Space Exodus*) are glossy, beautifully stylized dystopian shorts. These fictions are often experimental in narrative strategy and/or exhibition context. Sansour has noted that

DOI: 10.4324/9781003474449-4

her turn to science fiction coincided with the Second Intifada.[8] The incredibility of the real drove her toward dystopian science fiction as a space through which to explore Palestinian experience. Her earlier film work engaged humorously with questions of food and cultural identity or drew on pop culture tropes to highlight the Palestinian situation. For example, in *Bethlehem Bandolero* (2004), Sansour performs in a sombrero as a gunslinger in a shoot off with the wall in the occupied territories, and in *Happy Days* (2005), she casts herself as "The Palestinian," performing in a montage of scenes depicting daily life in the OPT, counterpointed by the bubbly theme song from the American sitcom that gives the film its title.

Since *A Space Exodus* Sansour has primarily worked in collaboration with her partner, Danish philosopher and writer Søren Lind, with whom she usually shares directorial credit. Her film installations are often augmented by plastic arts. For example, a room containing a large black sphere, entitled *Monument for Lost Time*, accompanied the film *In Vitro* (2019) at the Venice Biennale. *In the Future* was accompanied by *Archaeology in Absentia* (2016), "a sculptural installation of fifteen 20cm bronze munition replicas."[9] Each munition replica contained a disc engraved with the coordinates to sites where porcelain plates had been buried. Sanour's earlier film *A Space Exodus* was accompanied by a group of Palestinian astronaut figures, 30 cm tall, which she called *Palestinauts*.

Sansour's move into dystopic science fiction began with the aforementioned trilogy of *A Space Exodus*, *Nation Estate* and *In the Future They Ate from the Finest Porcelain*, and her following films build on this work thematically and aesthetically. The dystopic thrust has continued in *In Vitro* and *As If No Misfortune Had Occurred in the Night* (2022). All of these films remove Palestinian experience from contemporary Palestine, spatially and/or temporally. The structuring absence of Israel and Palestine as *named* entities, particularly from *In the Future* onward, has the effect of distilling the experience of occupation time and space via their speculative re-presentation. They stage a decolonial imaginary where the trauma and complexity of Palestinian experience is negotiated without the material or manifest presence of the colonizer. This also has the effect of rendering a very specific subject (settler colonial history in Palestine) more generalizable: the Palestinian condition increasingly becomes not only the basis for thinking through *Palestinian* relationships to time, history and memory in her work but is also a microcosm that reflects on identity, erasure and disaster more broadly. As noted in the introduction, Sansour's work moves toward larger questions of environmental collapse, memory and trauma, in ways that are both localized and at the same time have much broader implications, opening the possibility of transnational connection and challenging modern/colonial constructions of time and space.

Sansour's work contributes to a decolonization of the science fiction genre, which has historically been dominated by Western (and male) perspectives.[10]

One interviewer paraphrases Sansour's observation that "more powerful states like the USA and the UK have used SF to dominate the public imaginary with their narratives, while marginalised groups are represented by documentaries, being seen through anthropological lenses."[11] This reduction to ethnographic documentary is countered in Sansour's art practice, as are conventional divisions between fact and fiction. She says of her work, "I attempt to create scenarios where the Palestinian is no longer the victim, but instead enjoys the same power as anyone else in our media-driven, entertainment-led world."[12] Jussi Parikka argues that for many non-Western artists working in the genre (including Sansour) "science fiction becomes a way to articulate the necessity to think of futures as part of a horizon of struggles and the historical awareness [of] past futurisms alongside already existing ones."[13] Parikka uses the concept of *counterfuturism* to describe these works. Counterfuturism is a decolonial practice in which,

> instead of mourning a lost future, . . . turn[s] to looking at conditions of time and temporality as central to the functioning of power, mapping the situations in which futurity is important for current practices of living and exploring the ways in which an analysis of dislocations of identity and time can become more than dystopic representations.[14]

If modernity and colonialism are inextricably linked, then the constructions of time they have relied on for their power are in need of decolonial revision. Time as a linear narrative in which civilization advances and spreads, or the ways in which time has been ordered and quantified in the industrial and then post-industrial periods, do not reflect the epistemic systems, worldviews and experiences of colonized peoples. As we will see in the following chapter, Basma Alsharif's reversed and cyclical constructions of time are one way of disrupting the temporal narrative of colonial modernity. This disruption also occurs in Manna's strategic repetitions of Palestinian history and here in Sansour's experiments in speculative futurism. Sansour reframes the mnemonic legacy of the past to disrupt revolutionary narratives and challenge ideas of progress, state nationalism and essentialized identity from a colonized and diasporic experience. El Shakry summarizes the concept of counterfuturism as "a temporal reconfiguration in which dystopic futures are recursively mediated through the past in existential negation of the conditions of the present."[15] In *Nation Estate*, we are shown an alternate future in which Palestine has been turned into a luxury highrise. Here, a dystopic imaginary draws on a history of occupation and conflict over territory, while offering an alternative, however unappealing, to the stagnation of the present.

Counterfuturism functions in tandem with the notion of Arabfuturism—a term coined in 2015 by Palestinian artist Sulaiman Majali in his Arabfuturist manifesto. The idea of Arabfuturism has roots in the idea of Gulf Futurism (2009) devised by Qatari-American artist Sophia Al Maria, which itself takes inspiration from Afrofuturist thinking, artmaking and worldbuilding.[16] Lama Suleiman's paralleling of Palestinian art practices with Afrofuturism is worth quoting at length here, as it speaks to some key features of Sansour's practice:

> From a Palestinian readership perspective, Afrofuturism conjures echoes of lived experiences and collective memories that relate to Afrofuturistic threads such as the *apocalypse* that has already happened, the unattainable *return* to the *normal*, power regimes of colonialism, racism, marginalization, displacement, and collective identities of self-victimization.[17]

The apocalypse that has already happened and the unattainable return to the normal read as descriptions of major thematic concerns of *In the Future, In Vitro* and *As If No Misfortune Had Occurred in the Night*. Just as Suleiman argues that "Third World" futurisms "can offer diasporic cultures a way to deconstruct and reconstruct history in a manner that infiltrates territorial and mental borders," in his manifesto, Majali argues that Arabfuturism is explicitly linked to a postnational imaginary: "Arabfuturism is accelerating the transformation of representation; beyond the logic of the state." That Arabfuturism "bulldozes cultural nostalgias that prop up a dubious political paralysis" seems particularly apposite to Sansour's increasingly dominant thematic preoccupations with memory and trauma as forces that can hold back the very futures they so desire.

Sansour's work counters colonialist (i.e., Orientalist) representation with Palestinian futurisms, and static notions of identity with something in process and open to reimagining. As Said has thoroughly demonstrated, the Zionist project relied heavily on orientalist discourse in legitimating and garnering support for itself.[18] The European Jew was to be a civilizing force in an area of the world populated by a barbaric and backward people, Muslim decadents who were (by the second half of the 20th century) at risk of turning communist. Sansour's counterfuturisms, with their hypermodern aesthetic, beautiful attention to detail in mise-en-scène and costume and playful iconography, offer counterimages of Palestinian technological competence (her characters are astronauts, master botanists, expert forgers of historical artifacts). *As If No Misfortune Had Occurred in the Night* is an opera and offers a visually stunning and sonically lush instance of Palestinian identity narrated through a predominantly European high cultural form. These futurisms are distinctly Palestinian with much broader ramifications; they offer dystopian visions that don't merely reproduce Western sci-fi tropes but decolonize them by offering a perspective from the *damnées*.

In thinking through the feminist dimensions of this practice, it seems significant that all of Sansour's films feature women. In fact, there are no male speaking characters in the group of films considered here. In *A Space Exodus* and *Nation Estate*, it is Sansour herself who stars, and in the latter film, the protagonist is pregnant. Interestingly, this detail is almost never mentioned by commentators on the film.[19] Sansour has said:

> It is very important for me to have female voices and figures be central in my work. The female perspective is important in dismantling the given accepted structures that humanity has long lived with and that are of course often built by centuries of patriarchal thought and governing systems. Just like many elements in my work, the female figure becomes another post-structuralist tool for dismantling narratives.[20]

According to Aaron Rosenfeld, feminist dystopian narratives

> are more likely to include the possibility of other worlds and to focus not on the backward-orientated nostalgia of the last man, but on a forward-orientated first woman figure, for whom a change in the status quo is as likely to be promising as threatening.[21]

This resonates with a Post-Third-Worldist sensibility in which an attachment to nationhood or ethnic identity may not be the same for women (or gender and sexual minorities) as for men, when culture itself needs to be radically rethought on the basis of fundamental equality. Sansour's work negotiates not necessarily nostalgia, but the role history and memory play in identity while positing futures in which women are central players.

The Story of Nonel and Vovel (2009), a collaboration with London-based Israeli artist Oreet Ashery, is worth outlining here before turning to the films because it illustrates some of the major concepts and themes in Sansour's work.[22] The graphic novel is a metanarrative in which alteregos of the artists (called Nonel and Vovel) are infected by a substance that will destroy their artistic abilities in exchange for superpowers. They are offered a choice whether to proceed with the effects of the virus or to return to being artists. Although the women decide they want to stay artists (after much discussion about art, money, labor and politics), they find out that they never really had a choice. The virus is irreversible. Resigned to superhero status, Nonel (Ashery) and Vovel (Sansour) decide to take on settler colonialism in the OPT as their first mission. Once they arrive, they discover that a group of local female ninjas are already dealing with the situation on the ground and have information that the two artists lack. At this point we can already see the emphasis on speculative scenarios as powerful conduits for reimagining the present and opening up an alternate future that may seem hopeless or foreclosed in the current moment. We can also see the foregrounding of women (and artists!) as countermodels to the typical fighter, hero or leader of political revolution. In the story, Aida, the head ninja, tries to explain that there is something much bigger than the occupation going on that the two (former) artists don't understand.

Sansour's alterego, Vovel, challenges Aida, concerned she is denying the reality of the occupation. Aida reassures her, "don't worry about the occupation. It's real alright. But it's not just an occupation. It's a cover-up for an operation of much more terrifying proportions."[23] Here, we see Palestine as an instance of and occasion for speculating on broader global problems, which in the story are galactic. As Aida explains, there is a fifth planet, ruled by a villainous mastermind, a cosmic colonizer. The fifth planet is in fact "a nomadic planet relocating every time the soil of the minor planet it annexes is exhausted."[24] Earth is being prepared as the next host planet, and Palestine is being developed as a walled-in container to store fertilizer for the aliens' strange diet. The story turns Israel and its ally, the United States, into "powerless puppets" working unbeknownst to themselves in the interests of the fifth planet.[25] In this sense the novel steps back from the immediacy of the occupation to make space for thinking about what kinds of change are most meaningful, about the most urgent current issues we face (for Palestinians and the world more generally) and about what kind of world we want to live in.

At the story's end, the two artists (in a metareflection on the superhero narrative in the novel) speculate about the premature ending—the evil intergalactic villain is defeated, but peace remains elusive in the occupied territories. Should the heroes have continued on to solve the question of Palestine? Sansour's alterego comments, "it would have been tremendously gratifying to see vital changes brought about. Fiction or no fiction."[26] These last words signal another recurring preoccupation in her work: the irreality of reality for Palestinians, inextricable from the discursive hegemony of Israeli historical myths and present political fictions. Sansour moves into a post-factual[27] mode in her work, opening a space for more equitable exploration.

In what follows, I'll divide Sansour's dystopian work into two sections, in the process breaking up the aforementioned "trilogy." First, I briefly discuss *A Space Exodus* and *Nation Estate* in relation to their decolonial strategies, particularly around notions of space, connecting them with some other Palestinian video work. Second, I move to *In the Future*, *In Vitro*, and *As If No Misfortune Had Occurred in the Night*. In these works, while space is still a prevalent theme, time becomes foregrounded, and with it issues of memory, identity and the uses of history.

Place and (Outer) Space in *A Space Exodus* (2009) and *Nation Estate* (2012)

Sansour herself is the star of both *A Space Exodus* and *Nation Estate*, continuing a tradition from her earlier non-science fiction work. In *A Space Exodus*, she is costumed as a Palestinian astronaut (Figure 4.1). Over the ship's radio we hear, "Jerusalem we have a problem," followed by the reassurance that "No, everything is fine. We are back on track." Her astronaut successfully lands on the moon, planting a Palestinian flag: "That's one small step for

Figure 4.1 Palestinian space in *A Space Exodus* (2009).

Palestinians, one giant leap for mankind." The film suggests that Palestinian liberation is necessarily connected to a larger metric of humanity's progress. The soundtrack draws on the classical compositions used in Stanley Kubrick's *2001: A Space Odyssey* but inflects them with instrumentation and percussion characteristic of Arab folk music, including ululations. Like Sansour's spacesuit, which is marked by traditional Arabian details such as upward-pointing toes on the footwear, the soundtrack alerts us to the cultural specificity of this otherwise universally iconic action. That the astronaut here is a Palestinian *woman* also adds to the film's revision of the *2001* narrative. Despite claiming this small victory for Palestine, the astronaut finally floats away into space, while a voice questioningly calls out "Jerusalem? Jerusalem?" Here, a Palestinian experience of space is evoked in the elusive attempt to claim territory. The feeling of being catapulted without tether into the galaxy evokes the diasporic experience. That the refugee or diasporic Palestinian is a sleek astronaut with the technological competence to travel through space presents a decolonial counterimage through which to think Palestinian experiences of space and territorial belonging.

A more recent film by Mona Benyamin, *Moonscape* (2020), shares these themes with *A Space Exodus*. Both films use humor to explore Palestinian dispossession and dislocation. *Moonscape* is shot like a music video, the screen continuously branded in the corner with the label "Song of Hope." Hope has multiple meanings here, as the film is about the hope represented by real estate on the moon or the ability to buy a "Lunar Embassy" passport, and hope also references the founder of the Lunar Embassy, whose name (ironically) is

Dennis M. Hope. The Arabic song recounts Hope's story, an American who claimed the right to sell shares of the moon and other non-Earth planets in 1980, after discovering a loophole in the 1967 UN Space Treaty (incidentally, not a good year for Palestine or its neighboring countries). The treaty text is quoted on the screen: "Outer space, including the Moon and other celestial bodies, is not subject to national appropriation by claim of sovereignty, by means of use or occupation, or by any other means." While Israel was illegally occupying a collection of territories in 1967, the UN was occupied with protecting outer space from imperialism. Since Hope is an individual rather than a nation-state, he proceeded to copyright *his* claim to outer space.

Moonscape is full of irony. The song lyrics observe that "It is more possible for a Palestinian at Ain Al-Hilweh refugee camp [in Lebanon], who has access to the internet, to buy an acre or even 20 on the moon than to return to their homeland." Meanwhile, as a Palestinian with Israeli citizenship, Benyamin cannot travel to Lebanon. The film's black and white aesthetic is quasi-Lynchian (Figure 4.2). Benyamin's camped up parents perform the song for the camera, joined by a parrot and a computer-generated dancing alien, intercut with stock space imagery. Inserted throughout are screenshots of Benyamin's email exchanges with the Lunar Embassy. In these letters, she tries to assess the hopefulness of Palestinians and the citizens of other countries according to whether they have purchased outer space real estate; she speculates that buying this land is an indication of hopefulness. The moon, she notes to the Lunar Embassy, is a symbol for "a different future." It is revealed that of Palestine, Lebanon, Syria, Iraq, Jordan, Morocco, Algeria, Tunisia, Egypt, Saudi Arabia, Qatar, the United Arab Emirates (UAE) and Israel, only Saudi Arabia, the

Figure 4.2 Lynchian Camp and Music Video Aesthetics in Benyamin's *Moonscape* (2020).

UAE and Israel have seen a handful of sales over the past few years. Any hope the film raises about a peaceful off-planet existence is dampened somewhat by the revelation that customers frequently ask the Lunar Embassy staff what can be done if they do not like their new neighbors.

Benyamin wonders if a Lunar Embassy passport will allow her to enter Lebanon, which her Israeli passport currently makes impossible. Dr. Hope suggests she carry the two passports and get them both stamped when crossing terrestrial borders: "After 5 stamps she may be able to enter other countries with [the Lunar Embassy Passport]." She decides to try this, but the film ends on a less hopeful note: in the address section of the Lunar Embassy passport, Benyamin's birth country is listed as Israel. Although the singer's mother had promised her an acre of land "far from the reach of colonialism," even the Lunar Embassy cannot escape the colonial-nationalist politics that govern her mobility.

I've gone into a bit of detail about *Moonscape* here to establish a pattern of concerns that resonate between Sansour and a younger filmmaker, like Benyamin. Interrogating Palestinian experiences of space and identity, they turn to outer space, drawing on futurist aesthetics to reflect humorously on the impossibility of the present situation for Palestinians (whose realities vary, as evidenced in the contrast between a refugee from Ain Al-Hilweh who can't enter Palestine and a Palestinian Israeli citizen who can't cross the border the other way). Chrisoula Lionis connects a rise in the use of humor in contemporary Palestinian art and film to a "decline in nationalist hope following Oslo."[28] Lionis argues that the international media's saturation with images of Palestinian suffering, which became the only way Palestinians were ever seen (i.e., as victims), produced a "trauma fatigue" that Palestinian artists respond to with humor, where humor "intimates an understanding of laughter's ability to unhinge the latent oppression in the international gaze"[29] and "can reveal the perversity of our gaze, while shielding against it."[30] Perhaps most significantly, she suggests that "humour acts as an anticipatory action" that imagines the future of Palestine.[31] In the work of Sansour and Benyamin, humor, resilience, persistence and a creative commitment to exploring Palestinianness through new conceptual and aesthetic modes enact a decolonial Palestinian futurism.

Sansour's next film, *Nation Estate*, like *Moonscape* and *A Space Exodus*, is concerned with the politics of space and draws on a dystopian futurism. In the film, Palestine has become a sleek highrise, funded by international interests. Sansour's character travels by subway, escalator and elevator to the floor of Bethlehem (Figure 4.3). Airport-style announcements echo through the speakers; the elevator informs us that Norwegian Fjords is the supporter of "this week's general water supply" and advertises the sushi at Gaza Shore, "located on the Mediterranean floor." Floors are devoted to cities such as Bethlehem and Ramallah, as well as the Dead Sea, a Souq, nongovernmental organizations, the Olive Grove and Vertical Urban Planning. Floor lobbies

Figure 4.3 Larissa Sansour's *Nation Estate* (2012).

include replicas of key architectural monuments and ancient ruins. This postapocalyptic, sanitized and highly commodified Palestine is still a tightly controlled space—the inhabitants appear to wear standardized uniforms, the Palestinian flag adorns their access card to different spaces in the building and ads remind them of the necessity of having their documents validated for travel. As Eyal Weizman described in *Hollow Land: Israel's Architecture of Occupation*, Israel as a political space is "one desperately struggling to separate the inseparable, by attempting to multiply a single territorial reality and create two insular national geographies that occupy the same space."[32] The film seems to take as its conceptual inspiration that "With it, the imaginary spaces of conflict have seemingly fully adopted the scale of a building, resembling a complex architectural construction, perhaps an airport, with its separate inbound and outbound levels, security corridors, and many checkpoints."[33] After preparing one of many self-heating traditional meals in her characterless laboratory-like apartment unit (complete with olive tree), the pregnant character looks out on the "real" Jerusalem, on the other side of the still-present wall, as she cradles her stomach. As mentioned, her pregnancy is rarely noted in discussions of the film; I highlight it here to establish a pattern in Sansour's work of connecting questions of futurity, identity and cultural transmission to a matriarchal line.

This dystopian "solution" relies on the commodification of Palestinian culture and history, removed from their connection with community and the land, presumably still occupied by Israel. It suggests that the symbols and icons of Palestinianness themselves are not sufficient for forging a dimensional sense of self, and it critiques a sterilized vision of the future supported by neocolonial structures of aid. In this way, it reframes the question of Palestinian identity—its relationship to space and its controlling images—and invites a futurist reimagining of Palestinian political aims.

Palestinian Women Talking: Memory and Trauma in *In the Future They Ate from the Finest Porcelain* (2016), *In Vitro* (2019), and *As If No Misfortune Had Occurred in the Night* (2022)

In the Future They Ate from the Finest Porcelain acts as a hinge point between the largely spatial imaginaries of *Space Exodus* and *Nation Estate* and an increasing thematic focus on temporality as it connects to memory and history. While space continues to be an important consideration in Sansour's work, these films with Lind have foregrounded identity through time and its relationship to traumatic intergenerational histories. The protagonist of *In the Future* manipulates the age of pottery before burying it, in order to ensure Palestinians a future claim to the land via archaeological proof of historical residence. A dialogue between the protagonist, leader of the resistance, and a psychiatrist, both women, accompanies the film's dystopian postmodern imagery. The visuals are primarily staged in a hyperreal desert, where live action combines with historical collage, as figures from various periods in the history of Palestine populate the scenes (Figure 4.4).

Figure 4.4 The resistance leader alongside historical figures in *In the Future They Ate from the Finest Porcelain* (2016).

In the Future also features recurring images of the resistance leader walking through darkness, of she and her sister as children and of a floating white object, which at times appears to be her hospital bed and at others a metaphoric coffin, in which her (now dead) sister lies (Figure 4.5).

The film repurposes biblical imagery, from ships that look like a plague of locusts and "a porcelain monsoon like a biblical plague," to references to the Shroud of Turin and an image of the resistance leader at a table surrounded by various historical figures that evokes The Last Supper (see Figure 4.4). Many pasts seem to communicate with the present in these images, but the psychiatrist insists that the resistance leader's historical interventions are futile. "You're devoting your life to communicating with the past and future, but it's impossible," she says. The protagonist counters with profound *sumud*: she is willing to wait hundreds of years for her intervention to be unearthed.

Sansour and Lind's next collaboration, the dystopian two-channel video *In Vitro*, is also a dialogue between two women. In the wake of an oil-related environmental disaster, people have relocated underground. A bedridden older biologist, Dunia (played by Hiam Abbas), central to organizing the reproduction of flora and fauna that will repopulate the earth above when it is safe again, converses with a clone of her daughter, Alia (played by Maisa Abd Elhadi), who has been implanted with false memories of the time before (Figure 4.6).[34] Shot in crisp black and white, the film focuses on the two women conversing inside the architecturally stunning bunker—Dunia lies in her hospital bed, while Alia perambulates around the room. In addition to images of the film's

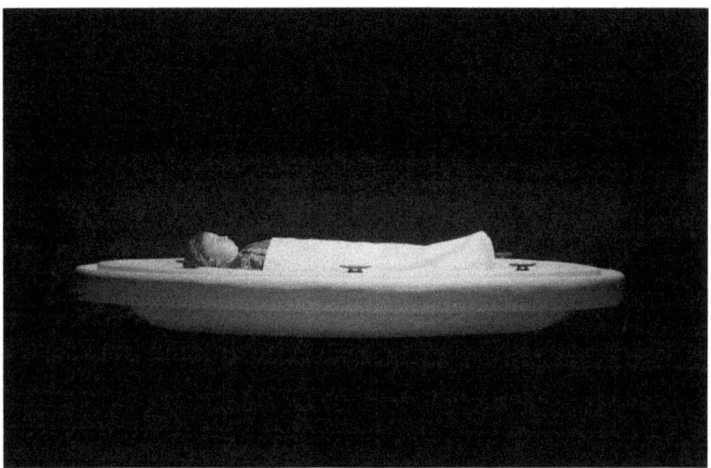

Figure 4.5 The resistance leader's martyred sister in the white object.

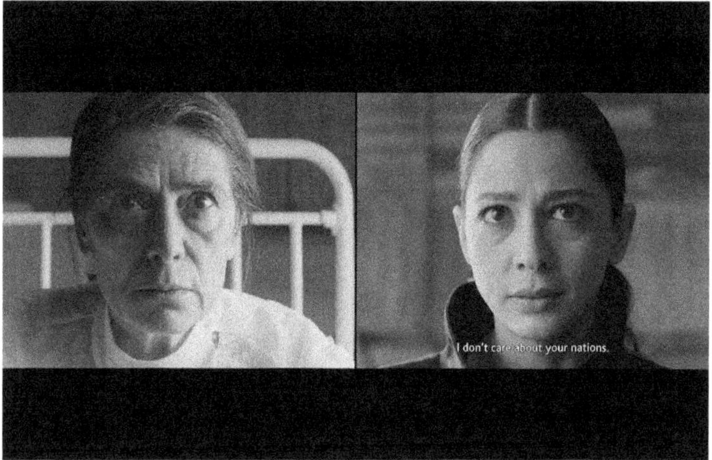

Figure 4.6 Dunia and Alia in *In Vitro* (2019).

present, periodically, one of the two video channels shows archival footage from various moments in pre-1967 Bethlehem, including the forced displacement of Palestinians. Like the images of oil flooding Bethlehem that begin the film, or those from Alia's pre-catastrophe childhood that occur throughout, these are impossible memories/images that have been passed on to the daughter's clone.

Finally, *As If No Misfortune Had Occurred in the Night* is a three-channel video that stages similar themes of apocalypse and personal trauma through an operatic monologue (Figure 4.7). The three channels evoke a religious tryptic—the center panel is the largest, with two narrower panels on either side. Only one woman, the singer (Nour Darwish), is present in the film, whose settings vary from an abandoned church, to an abstracted forest of branches suspended from above, to several minimalist, stylized spaces clearly set on a soundstage. At one point, the singer enters a pool of liquid that dyes her white robe a dark blue in the otherwise black and white film. Based on Mahler's *Kindertotenlieder* and the traditional Palestinian song *Al Ouf Mash'al*, the singer mourns the death of her daughter. Many of the lyrics are taken directly from the Mahler song cycle, but translated into Arabic, such as:

> Now the sun will rise as brightly
> As if no misfortune had occurred in the night
> A little light has been extinguished in my household
> The misfortune has fallen on me alone

Figure 4.7 Nour Darwish in *As If No Misfortune Had Occurred in the Night* (2022).

The traditional lyrics are combined with new lyrics, written by Lind, that communicate a Palestinian experience of temporality and trauma:

> I mourn not only the losses I can count
> But also those ahead and yet unnumbered
> Each tragedy shared with those still unborn
> My blood delivering the words
> I forbid myself to speak

Here the lyrics speak of ongoing and vicarious intergenerational trauma, passed on through the body. Each scene has a stark feeling, with underpopulated settings adding to the impression of a world barely persisting after catastrophe. While the protagonist in *Nation Estate* is expecting a child, *In the Future* is haunted by the death of a younger sister. By *In Vitro*, the daughter has been lost and then reproduced in clone form. In *As If No Misfortune*, the daughter is irrevocably gone, and the singer's grief feels endless. Although the film doesn't have a science fiction "plot" per se, its stylized mise-en-scène and postapocalyptic setting place it firmly in the lineage of Sansour and Lind's earlier dystopian futurist works. The soundtrack, by Lebanese composer Anthony Sahyoun, contributes to this futurism. Sayhoun is known for his synth compositions, which electronically process and modify instruments. His composition for the film is layered and rich, with periods that sound like more traditional opera instrumentation and others that move into the realm of sound effects, such as creaking, shutting or rustling. These often foreboding and ominous combinations contribute to the cinematic quality of the audio design. Throughout, Sayhoun's synth creations become glitchy, at times evoking reverberations of digital debris. The soundtrack thus both further connects the Arabic lyrics to European and Palestinian music traditions and also moves beyond them, into a digital future.

As in Afrofuturist narratives, the apocalypse has already happened in all of these films, and what is experienced in Palestine has actually made Palestinians more prepared for the dystopian future that is on the horizon for all, should humanity continue on its current course. In *In the Future*, the resistance leader opines, "This place was always a barely functioning dystopia. Deeper into the apocalypse, an accelerated microcosm." In *In Vitro*, Dunia similarly narrates that "Elsewhere eventually caught up and had their own doomsday," implying the Palestinian experience was merely a harbinger of future global events. "Others were beginning to experience what we had seen for years." The anywhere and anyplace quality of *As If No Misfortune* suggests broader relevance for its story of recurring trauma, stored in the body and passed through generations. The protagonist sings of her experience of time, "With everything at a standstill tomorrow cedes its place/To endless repetitions of waiting in vain." Reem Fadda sees the condition of stagnation as particularly germane to broader experiments in futurist thinking. In her written response to *The Novel of Nonel and Vovel*, she notes that the "state of stagnation and digress . . . is an open space for contemplation in order to answer existential dilemmas that are not just for the Palestinians or the Israelis."[35] Again, this notion of Palestine-as-microcosm is reinforced by the fact that Palestine (or Israel) is never explicitly named in these works. The films also further develop Sansour's interest in the permeable and sometimes irrelevant boundary between fact and fiction.

The protagonist of *In the Future* calls herself a "narrative terrorist": just as Manna's foragers waged a discursive war around land rights and sustainability, Sansour's resistance leader fights against Israeli territorial claims rooted in (selective) archaeology. She explains to her psychiatrist, "Myth not only creates fact, it also generates identification." She fights fire with fire, myth with countermyth. "[R]eality in some cases could become so fictional that the only way to address it is to make work that exaggerates it even more," Sansour has commented.[36] The resistance leader's act of remythologization is reinforced by Sansour-as-artist in the aforementioned exhibit, *Archaeology in Absentia*, a companion to the film. Again, the work is a series of 15 bronze sculptures: replicas of munitions measuring 20 cm. Discs inside of each capsule contain the geographical coordinates to locations where plates have been buried in Palestine. As in the film, these plates are hand-painted with Palestinian patterns. Although Sansour has ceded the lead role here to an actor, she, like the narrative terrorist, makes/buries her own history.

In Vitro also probes the role of fiction in state- and identity-building. Dunia argues that "Entire Nations are built on fairy tales. Facts alone are too sterile for a cohesive understanding." Within both films, the characters offer different perspectives on history and futurity. In *In Vitro*, the different rhetorical positions taken up by the women concern the role of memory, rituals and symbols of the past and their relationship to the future for generations who have never known life before the disaster. Alia represents a younger generation pushing back on the way their lives have been defined by their parents' trauma *and* their attempted solutions. Conversing with the bed-ridden Dunia, Alia struggles with memories that she hasn't herself experienced. "I despise the idea of the present as nothing but a void," she says. Dunia seems to concur:

> This present barely exists. You were born into purgatory, like past generations in this place. They all tried to redeem their present, lit up with old stories and decorated the void with promises of things to come. But the void only grows. Soon, it's so imposing and violent it devours everything in its way.

Alia rejects an identity linked to nationalism and rooted in *ressentiment*, which can't be lived *now* and *here*, "I don't care about your nations. Their stories, their rituals, their repetition of imagery. . . . Memory channeled by a handful of tropes." Alia, like the narrative terrorist of *In the Future*, wants to act; she is tired of waiting. There is a sense that the past is holding her back. Visually, the two-channel structure creates a profound mirroring effect between the women. Dunia and Alia both face the camera in close-up in their respective channels, giving the viewer a simultaneous shot/reverse shot that visually reinforces a gap between the women's perspectives through the thin black bar dividing the two screens (see Figure 4.6). The form poses questions of identity and generational inheritance, visually underlining the themes of the dialogue. Sometimes, the daughter circumnavigates the area where her mother rests, one channel showing her back and the other her front, creating a feeling of circularity that is reinforced in other scenes by the prisonlike multi-floored circular bunker she traverses (Figure 4.8).

Whereas *In Vitro* is explicitly an intergenerational dialogue, in *In the Future*, the age difference between interlocutors is unclear. The psychiatrist in *In the Future* wants to explain the resistance leader's actions by her personal trauma (her sister was killed at the age of nine). For the psychiatrist, there is a stable meaning, a certain logic that can be discovered beneath the symptoms of the present. The resistance leader refuses to explain the political in terms of the personal alone—hers is perhaps a more radical approach, rooted in action and focused on a dream for the future as opposed to reconciliation with the past. The women debate the relationship between personal trauma and political action, between past trauma and the present, and the impact of present action on the future. While clearly affected by the murder of her sister, the protagonist refuses to read her own actions purely as a *reaction* to this personal trauma. Her intervention is rooted in generative acts and not simply reactivity.

Figure 4.8 Circular Motifs in *In Vitro* (2019).

She insists on a larger political reading of her sister's death: "They mistook her for something else. They didn't know what they killed. At a certain point death is no longer about the single life lost. It is not even personal. It's what we are as a whole that qualifies us as targets."

In *In Vitro*, trauma is also explicitly acknowledged, as both a personal and collective phenomenon. Alia's trauma, unlike that of the narrative terrorist, is inherited trauma that functions via postmemory. It is not her own experiences that have led to the frozen present but rather those experienced by and inherited from prior generations. Typically, in discussions of postmemory, trauma is understood as passed on through the emotions, stories, silences and images of parents or a previous generation.[37] In *In Vitro*, trauma has been scientifically reproduced in Alia in the form of memories/images of the disaster. This produces a speculative scenario for replicating the effects of postmemory, in which "experiences were transmitted to [those affected] so deeply and affectively as to seem to constitute memories in their own right."[38] Significantly for film and visual media, it is via *images* that postmemory is often transmitted: *In Vitro* evokes this via fabricated and archival images of life before and during the disaster. Dunia implores Alia, "We need you to guard these images." "Memories," Alia corrects. Dunia then muses, "I'm no longer sure what they are." The images, as in the workings of postmemory, are performative rather than indexical links to the past. They erupt in the channel next to the present, just as trauma collapses temporal distinctions.

The traumatic disaster in the diegesis is of course the oil spill that floods the streets of Bethlehem in the film's opening imagery, but it also refers to *The*

Disaster (*al-Nakba*) for Palestinians (Figure 4.9). With respect to the film's emphasis on environmental catastrophe, it also reflects what E. Ann Kaplan has labeled "pretrauma" in her work on climate disaster films.[39] "If in classic trauma, subjects 'act out' instead of 'working through' catastrophes from the past, in pretrauma subjects are haunted by what they fear is coming from the future."[40] This future haunting relates specifically to the imminence of environmental catastrophe in Kaplan's research. The temporality of *In Vitro* draws on both past traumas that have occurred in the viewer's world (1948, 1967 . . . 2023) and also on the environmental collapse that viewers fear in the future. Nat Muller reads the film's emphasis on environmental collapse as a kind of "memory for the future."[41] It is worth noting that in the group of dystopian climate disaster films that Kaplan studies, the hero is typically a white male,[42] who saves women and children (of any race) by the film's end.[43] In *In Vitro*, it is unclear that either of the two characters is a hero in line with conventional archetypes, but both women evince a strength and persistence that may guarantee humanity a future. The film thus centers two Arab women with the ability and competence to preserve and guard the past, as well as determine the future, in contradistinction to the vast majority of films in the pretrauma genre (another decolonial intervention). While Kaplan notes that the patterns she identifies in climate disaster cinema may be due to the fact that white men have the most to lose in the case of environmental collapse, the focus shifts here, onto Palestinian women whose experiences have prepared them for the collapse of the world long before it took place. We can look to *them* for a way forward, not because they have the most to lose, but because they

Figure 4.9 The catastrophe in *In Vitro* (2019).

bear deep wisdom when it comes to losing and rebuilding. This also gestures to the larger reach of the films (Palestine-as-microcosm), as well as the way they move beyond the nation-state (or lack thereof) as the primary focal point and toward issues of global sustainability, much as we saw in *The Novel of Nonel and Vovel.*

As noted, *As If No Misfortune* also centers the theme of trauma, with the singer describing its presence within her body, both inherited and experienced firsthand: "My cells are imbibed with the clicks of a gun/Each violent instant lodged in my codes." She has passed this on to her daughter, lamenting, "The cataclysm of a century ago revisited in eternal sequels/ Paying off their losses for decades yet to come/ Each possible future shackled by a past/Embedded deep within you, too, far beyond my reach." As in *In Vitro*, the use of archival images in *As If No Misfortune* suggests the temporal confusions of trauma, as well as the functioning of postmemory. The film frequently uses black screens as a way of indicating ruptures in the present. Images of the past do not appear alongside those of the present moment, as they do in *In Vitro*, but instead occur during breaks in the singing. Here, it is as if the traumatic images fill a space unoccupiable by the linear flow of narration, emerging where language leaves a void.

Beyond Trauma Time

Connected to traumatic temporalities, but also moving beyond them, the films present nonlinear temporalities that have deeper implications for their futurist imaginaries. The past as archival images in *In the Future* occur in the form of collage figures populating the desert. Past and present exist simultaneously for the protagonist, just as the two-channel structure of *In Vitro* allows mnemonic images to visually coexist with events set in the diegetic present. The collage format and the use of multiple channels evoke trauma time, in which the past constantly erupts into and is indistinguishable from the present. Trauma can result in an inability to fully exist in the now, and it is difficult to project a future from this psychological space. The *Nakba* is central to the traumatic conception of time in these pieces, as it is

> a key event in the Palestinian calendar—the baseline for personal histories and the sorting of generations. Moreover, it is the creator of an unsettled inner time. It deflects Palestinians from the flow of social time into their own specific history and often into a melancholic existence . . . or a ghostly nostalgia.[44]

Greg Burris has referred to this specifically Palestinian temporality as "Nakba time," since the *Nakba* is experienced as an ongoing catastrophe rather than an event discretely located in the past: "For the Palestinians, then, it is as if *time has stopped*, and the Nakba appears as a present and permanent condition."[45]

All of the Sansour/Lind films speak directly or indirectly of the present as a void or abyss, as a time of waiting, and of being haunted by the past with a future that seems always in abeyance. The singer in *As If No Misfortune* vocalizes Nakba time, "With everything at a standstill tomorrow cedes its place/ To endless repetitions of waiting in vain/ Days to come no different than those gone by/ Ejected from time and stripped of our chronology." This gestures to what Levy calls the syntagmatic relationship between Zionist and Palestinian temporality: with the establishment of Israel in Palestine, Zionists entered history/time, while Palestine and its people, the colonized, were ejected from history.[46] This construction relies on colonial narratives inseparable from the idea of modernity: the telos of Israel as nation-state depends on a discourse of the Palestinian as ahistorical.

Alia's rejection of "Their stories, their rituals, their repetition of imagery" resonates with Diana K. Allan's fieldwork in the Shatila camp. The standardization of images and narratives of the past, often centered around the *Nakba*, have formed a kind of "Palestinian identity canon," central to Palestinian politics. In her fieldwork, Allan felt compromised as an academic invested in archiving a particular history of displacement when she realized that many of the younger camp residents resented this focus on a singular defining past event. She notes that "The authenticity and legitimacy enacted—and often controlled—by this increasingly institutionalized understanding of 1948 history and its place within nationalist discourse clearly comes at a cost."[47] It "can be both alienating and oppressive," and "It is also replacing a sense of history as lived experience and practice that might evolve, organically, into future possibility."[48] *In Vitro* boldly puts these tensions on display, central to its decolonial futurist politics. It moves away from a solution to Palestinian trauma located in the nation-state as telos and shifts its focus to the survival of humanity as such. Circular motifs—such as the shape of the bunker building and Alia's circumnavigation of the space—suggest an entrapment in the past. Alia asks if, "Perhaps a loss of memories is essential to starting over?" By contrast, Dunia is worried about the past repeating itself if mistakes are forgotten. Alia wonders if "*next* time they won't be mistakes." Allan observes that it is not only older generations and academics who are invested in reproducing certain historical narratives but also NGOs, who often demand a focus on the past at the expense of encouraging children and others in the camps to reflect on their lives now and thus make the future available for creative dreaming (of nationalist belonging or otherwise).

Alia wants to replace the repetition of images and rituals with a forgetting that may allow repetitions with better results in the future. These are not repetitions that aim to achieve mastery over the traumatic past but to risk better futures. This play with temporalities of circularity and return is also a major theme of Alsharif's *Ouroboros*, discussed in the next chapter.

Paolo Jedlowski argues that

> memory is not only what serves the identity of a group and its present interests, but also the depository of traces that may be valid both in defetishizing the existing and in understanding the processes that have led to the present as it is now, and to the criticism of this very present in the name of forgotten desires, aspirations, or traumas.[49]

Manna's alternative archives and Nasser-Eldin's exploration of the nascent women's movement in 1929, both intervene in memory with the effects of "defetishizing the existing" and unearthing "forgotten desires, aspirations, or traumas." With similar results, but different methods, Sansour dreams futurist forms of the present in order to ask if memory is not open to other uses than the formation of a traumatic collective identity—what aspirations or desires may still be recuperable if time can be forgotten or rewritten?

If the films themselves contribute to a form of cultural memory work, they are part of a present that reframes the past, as does the character of the resistance leader. In *In Vitro* Dunia observes that her parents now look alike to her because she has seen them both in herself. The present changes the perspective on what came before: "At any given point, the present imposes its language . . . and projects the meaning of this very moment back onto the past," she explains. Memories can be altered, as can their meanings and uses. The dialectic between generational experiences of Palestinianness, isolated and amplified via a dystopian scenario in *In Vitro*, allows questions to be reposed about the past that unlock future possibilities. *In Vitro* materializes historical trauma in the form of a large black sphere that often appears in connection with footage of the past: it either introduces mnemonic images or appears in the channel next to them. In some scenes, Alia reaches out to touch the sphere, drawing closer to it, but it remains something opaque and impenetrable, an obstruction holding her back from her own future. In the film's installation at the Venice Biennale, the sphere (computer-generated in the film) was fabricated as a 5-meter-tall object, entitled *Monument to Lost Time*. Together, the film and sculptural installation formed a piece called *Heirloom*. As a physical monument, the history represented by the sphere is given its due memorialization, so the focus can shift to the Palestinian future.

While *In the Future's* postmodern collages of nuns, British colonial officers, Bedouins and other Palestinians suggest the collapsing of temporal (and spatial) difference typical of dreams or trauma, the title of the film suggests that a new way of thinking about temporality can emerge and replace "trauma time." By contrast with the time of trauma, the grammar of "in the future, they ate" suggests a form of future anteriority or a speculation on how the now relates to what will have been in the future. Tani Barlow has developed this concept in her history of 20th-century Chinese feminist writing.[50] Barlow reads particular invocations of "woman" as related not to a sense of what woman actually, stably signified at that moment in Chinese culture but as an invocation directed toward future generations. Here, I substitute the category of Palestinian for that of woman and the medium of videomaking for that of writing. Barlow argues that by thinking historiographically with the framework of future anteriority—what will have been—we can focus on "the politics of claiming" and "acts of invention."[51] This investment would shift from what Palestinianness *is* to how that identity is claimed and articulated in a given moment. This is in marked contrast to Jayussi's observation that in many oral histories of the *Nakba* narrators deploy the subjunctive future past tense, "a tensing within the past tense," "a knowing-now-what-it-was-all-going-to-amount-to, and a not-knowing-then-what-it-was-to-become."[52] This is a tense in which the present reflects on a past that is over and done, a tense of regret and of sobering hindsight. By contrast, the resistance leader, a younger generation, invokes the future anterior, in which the past does not determine the future but is actively being recreated in the name of future liberation. Similarly, Palestine and Palestinian are identities that are not only being referenced but also created and redefined through their invocation in these video works. Creative visions of Palestinianness and ways of thinking about Palestine offer new potentialities and a break with the stagnant experience of "Nakba time." I bring in Barlow here due to the particularly germane content of *In the Future*. The resistance leader is very aware that she is invoking a myth in order to redefine the past for the future. It matters less to her what Palestine is in the present than what it will have been in the future and how that will impact future political claims. She produces proof of a past *for* the future *from* the present: the film's title could just as well be *In the Future* They Will Have Eaten *from the Finest Porcelain*. As Barlow notes, "A history written in the future anterior . . . would not simply note the existence of a future encoded in every present, but would focus particularly on the capacity of this kind of present imagining to upset the sequence of past-present-future."[53] The leader of the resistance recognizes that fiction holds a stronger grip on geopolitics than does reality and fabricates her own historical intervention. Like Barlow's larger discussion of the category of woman as a "catachresis" or a term in search of a proper referent (that is to say, simply, a term whose meaning is not stable across time and place, but open to contestation and constantly in the process of being (re)defined), so too is the notion of Palestinian identity dessentialized in Sansour's work. Palestine and Palestinian as catachreses: what may seem a shift into relativity is framed as politically necessary for Alia and for the leader of the resistance.

Burris makes a related argument about the historical instability of all ethnic and national identifications. Interested in the ethical implications of Freud's argument in *Moses and Monotheism* that Moses was an Egyptian, rather than a Jew, and that there is thus a profound difference or otherness installed at the heart of Jewishness itself, he elaborates on Freud's "argument against the notion of ethnic, cultural or racial purity."[54] Noting that "Zionism represses Freud," Burris makes a parallel non-identitarian claim regarding Palestinianness:

> Unless those contesting the Israeli colonization and occupation of Palestine wish to replicate the hierarchical discourse and ideological framework of political Zionism, it is incumbent upon them to heed the lesson of Freud and recognize that, like the Jew, *the Palestinian does not exist.*[55]

For Burris, as the films discussed here appear to argue, what Palestine is and what it will have been in the future are entirely open to contestation: "there is no ontological foundation to Palestinian identity, and therefore, for the Palestinian, *nothing is impossible*. If the Zionist negation of Palestinian being aims to shut down possibilities, the affirmation of Palestinian non-existence opens them up."[56] These questions of identity permeate the dialogue of *In the Future*. The psychiatrist demands, "But by giving rise to this counterfeit people, aren't you accepting the erasure of your own?" While there is an inherited experience of Palestinianness for the protagonist, she refuses to accept a present defined entirely through victimhood and a future without hope. Palestine, then, is catachrestic: Palestine is a woman, an astronaut landing on the moon; Palestine is a narrative terrorist, rewriting the past for the future; Palestine is a clone, and it is also the woman who created the clone, rebuilding the future while contesting the past. In Manna's work, Palestinians are foragers, punks who disregard the colonial law, or a diverse set of music makers and mystics; Palestinians love to dress up in costume and party; they can be misogynist car-obsessed gym rats. Palestine is all these things, and, in many cases discussed here, Palestine is many places and many times, a microcosm of much larger issues facing the way we exist on the planet together.

Crucially, in these imaginings, Palestine is a mixed entity and not an ethnonationalist construct. This is well-illustrated by Sansour's installation, the *Monument to Lost Time*. The room in which the sphere was located also featured custom floor tiles. Sansour notes that the tile design

> incorporates tile motifs that figure in the film, which are not a traditional Palestinian design but early twentieth-century art nouveau style. In other words, a European pattern that, after being housed for over a century in the Ottoman villa in Bethlehem where *In Vitro* was filmed and later reinstalled in Venice takes on qualities of origin and authenticity.[57]

The tiles, like Lachmann's broadcasts, trouble the notion of pure national representation. Sansour saw the tiles as "part of the critique of essentialism when it comes to heritage."[58]

The story of *In Vitro* recalls a short story in which all of Gaza relocates underground.[59] In "The Underground Ghetto of Gaza" (2014) by Amir Nizar Zuabi, the narrator ends by musing about the above-ground, post-apocalyptic future. This is, crucially, a vision in which the future depends on our capacity to coexist with difference:

> And we start to hope that if we keep on digging, all the way to the core, if we don't stop, if we perforate the land like a honeycomb, if we make it as flimsy as silk, maybe it will suddenly collapse in on itself. And then, like a tray piled with cups of coffee and cookies that crashes to the floor in a mess of crumbs and glass, it will all mix together. The upper part and the lower part will blend. And the rules will change. And we'll be able to say with a sigh of relief: Here is a piece of sky mixed with a cracked piece of sea; here is Shujaiyeh mixed with Sderot; here is Zeitoun mixed with the Mount of Olives; here is compassion mixed with relief; here is one human being mixed with another. And we'll know that we were saved from the living death in which we are trapped, and now we'll join the life of above, and with them build a new land.

Notes

1 Lital Levy, "Temporalities of Israel/Palestine: Culture and Politics," *Critical Inquiry* 47 (Summer 2021): 695.
2 Levy, "Temporalities," 695.
3 Gil Z. Hochberg, *Becoming Palestine: Toward an Archival Imagination of the Future* (Durham: Duke University Press, 2021), 85.
4 Hochberg, *Becoming Palestine*, 86.
5 Nayrouz Abu Hatoum, "Decolonizing [in the] Future: Scenes of Palestinian temporality," *Geografiska Annaler: Series B, Human Geography* 103, no. 4 (2021): 400.
6 Hoda El Shakry, "Palestine and the Aesthetics of the Future Impossible," *Interventions: International Journal of Postcolonial Studies* 23, no. 5 (2021): 671.
7 El Shakry, "Palestine," 670.
8 Wafa Gabsi, "Fiction and Art Practice: Interview with Larissa Sansour 'A Space Exodus'," *Contemporary Practices* 10 (March 1, 2012).
9 Larissa Sansour, "Archeology in Absentia," *Larissa Sansour Website*, accessed May 17, 2023, https://larissasansour.com/Archaeology-in-Absentia-2017.
10 See, for example, Lore/tta LeMaster and Amber Johnson, "Speculative Fiction, Criticality, and Futurity: A Critical Introduction," *Communication and Critical/Cultural Studies* 18, no. 3 (2021).
11 The original interview is no longer available online, but is paraphrased in: "Interview with Larissa Sansour," *Vector*, March 31, 2018, accessed August 2, 2023, https://vector-bsfa.com/2018/03/31/interview-with-larissa-sansour/.
12 Gabsi, "Fiction and Art Practice," 115.

13 Jussi Parikka, "Middle East and Other futurisms: Imaginary Temporalities in Contemporary Art and Visual Culture," *Culture, Theory and Critique* 59, no. 1 (2018): 53.
14 Parikka, "Middle East," 55.
15 El Shakry, 670.
16 See Sophia Al-Maria, "The Gaze of Sci-Fi Wahabi," *The Gaze of Sci-Fi Wahabi*, 2008, accessed August 2, 2023, http://scifiwahabi.blogspot.com/.
17 Lama Suleiman, "Afrofuturism and Arabfuturism: Reflections of a Present-day Diasporic Reader," *Tohu*, June 12, 2016, accessed August 2, 2023, http://tohumagazine.com/article/afrofuturism-and-arabfuturism-reflections-present-day-diasporic-reader.
18 Edward W. Said, *The Question of Palestine* (New York: Vintage Books, 1979).
19 Parikka is the only scholar I've seen who remarks on this.
20 "Interview with Larissa Sansour."
21 Aaron S. Rosenfeld, *Character and Dystopia: The Last Men* (New York; London: Routledge, 2020). Quoted in Jade Hinchliffe, "Speculative Fiction, Sociology, and Surveillance Studies: Towards a Methodology of the Surveillance Imaginary," *Surveillance & Society* 19, no. 4 (2021): 418.
22 Oreet Ashery and Larissa Sansour, *The Novel of Nonel and Vovel* (New York: Charta, 2009). (Other artists and authors contributed as well, including Søren Lind, who wrote the text of the second of the two fictional stories.)
23 Ashery and Sansour, *Nonel and Vovel*, 146.
24 Ashery and Sansour, 149.
25 Ashery and Sansour, 149.
26 Ashery and Sansour, 168.
27 Labocine, "Envisioning Future States with Science Fiction," n.d., https://medium.com/labocine/envisioning-future-states-with-science-fiction-7a4ea54e00ca.
28 Chrisoula Lionis, *Laughter in Occupied Palestine: Comedy and Identity in Art and Film* (London: Bloomsbury, 2016), 17.
29 Lionis, *Laughter*, 147.
30 Lionis, 157.
31 Lionis, 157.
32 Eyal Weizman, *Hollow Land: Israel's Architecture of Occupation* (London; New York: Verso, 2017), 15.
33 Weizman, *Hollow Land*, 15.
34 The film was commissioned for the Danish Pavilion at the Venice Biennale, 2019.
35 Reem Fadda, "Not-Yet-Ness: Toward the Intergalactic," in *The Novel of Nonel and Vovel*, ed. Oreet Ashery and Larissa Sansour (New York: Charta, 2009), 171.
36 Gabsi, 115. See also El Shakry, on remythologization in the work.
37 Marianne Hirsch, *The Generation of Postmemory: Writing and Visual Culture After the Holocaust* (New York: Columbia University Press, 2012).
38 Marianne Hirsch. "The Generation of Postmemory," in *On Writing with Photography*, ed. Karen Beckman and Liliane Weissberg (Minneapolis: University of Minnesota Press, 2013), 205.

39 E. Ann Kaplan, *Climate Trauma: Foreseeing the Future in Dystopian Film and Fiction* (New Brunswick: Rutgers University Press, 2016).
40 E. Ann Kaplan. "Visualizing Climate Trauma: The Cultural Work of Films Anticipating the Future," in *The Routledge Companion to Cinema and Gender*, ed. Kristin Lené Hole, Dijana Jelača, E. Ann Kaplan, and Patrice Petro (London; New York: Routledge, 2017), 409.
41 Nat Muller. "Before and After a Disaster: Unsettling Representation in Larissa Sansour's 'Heirloom'," in *Research/Practice 03: Larissa Sansour Heirloom*, ed. Anthony Downey (London: Sternberg Press, 2019), 11.
42 Kaplan, "Visualizing Climate Trauma," 410.
43 Kaplan, 411.
44 Ahmad H. Sa'di and Lila Abu-Lughod, "Introduction: The Claims of Memory," in *Nakba: Palestine, 1948, and the Claims of Memory*, ed. Ahmad H. Sa'di and Lila Abu-Lughod (New York: Columbia University Press, 2007), 5.
45 Greg Burris, *The Palestinian Idea: Film, Media, and the Radical Imagination* (Philadelphia: Temple University Press, 2019), 87. Alia's position suggests this stagnation without growth in *In Vitro*. Dunia tells her, "You were born, but you are still trapped in the womb."
46 Levy, 684.
47 Diana K. Allan, "The Politics of Witness: Remembering and Forgetting 1948 in Shatila Camp," in *Nakba: Palestine, 1948, and the Claims of Memory*, ed. Ahmad H. Sa'di and Lila Abu-Lughod (New York: Columbia University Press, 2007), 257.
48 Allan, "Politics of Witness," 257.
49 Paolo Jedlowski, "Memory and Sociology: Themes and Issues," *Time and Society* 10, no. 1 (2001): 36. Quoted in Sa'di and Abu-Lughod, "Introduction," 6.
50 Tani Barlow, *The Question of Women in Chinese Feminism* (Durham: Duke University Press, 2004).
51 Barlow, *Question of Women*, 16.
52 Lena Jayussi, "Iterability, Cumulativity, and Presence: The Relational Figures of Palestinian Memory," in *Nakba: Palestine, 1948, and the Claims of Memory*, ed. Ahmad H. Sa'di and Lila Abu-Lughod (New York: Columbia University Press, 2007), 118.
53 Barlow, 17.
54 Burris, *Palestinian Idea*, 44.
55 Burris, 45.
56 Burris, 47.
57 Muller, "Before and After a Disaster," 17.
58 Lindsey Moore, "Suspended Between the Past and the Future: Larissa Sansour in Conversation with Lindsey Moore," in *Research/Practice 03: Larissa Sansour Heirloom*, ed. Anthony Downey (London: Sternberg Press, 2019), 129.
59 Amir Nizar Zuabi, "The Underground Ghetto City of Gaza," *Haaretz*, August 4, 2014, accessed May 22, 2023, www.haaretz.com/opinion/2014-08-04/ty-article/.premium/the-underground-ghetto-of-gaza/0000017f-e4dc-d9aa-afff-fddca82e0000?v=1678903419468.

Bibliography

Abu Hatoum, Nayrouz. "Decolonizing [in the] Future: Scenes of Palestinian Temporality." *Geografiska Annaler: Series B, Human Geography* 103, no. 4 (2021): 397–412.

Allan, Diana K. "The Politics of Witness: Remembering and Forgetting 1948 in Shatila Camp." In *Nakba: Palestine, 1948, and the Claims of Memory*, edited by Ahmad H. Sa'di and Lila Abu-Lughod, 253–82. New York: Columbia University Press, 2007.

Al-Maria, Sophia. "The Gaze of Sci-Fi Wahabi." *The Gaze of Sci-Fi Wahabi*, 2008. Accessed August 2, 2023. http://scifiwahabi.blogspot.com/.

Ashery, Oreet, and Larissa Sansour. *The Novel of Nonel and Vovel*. New York: Charta, 2009.

Barlow, Tani. *The Question of Women in Chinese Feminism*. Durham: Duke University Press, 2004.

Burris, Greg. *The Palestinian Idea: Film, Media, and the Radical Imagination*. Philadelphia: Temple University Press, 2019.

El Shakry, Hoda. "Palestine and the Aesthetics of the Future Impossible." *Interventions: International Journal of Postcolonial Studies* 23, no. 5 (2021): 669–90.

"Envisioning Future States with Science Fiction." *Labocine*. Accessed May 22, 2023. https://medium.com/labocine/envisioning-future-states-with-science-fiction-7a4ea54e00ca.

Fadda, Reem. "Not-Yet-Ness: Toward the Intergalactic." In *The Novel of Nonel and Vovel*, edited by Oreet Ashery and Larissa Sansour, 171–73. New York: Charta, 2009.

Gabsi, Wafa. "Fiction and Art Practice: Interview with Larissa Sansour 'A Space Exodus.' *Contemporary Practices* 10 (n.d.): 114–19.

Hirsch, Marianne. *The Generation of Postmemory: Writing and Visual Culture After the Holocaust*. New York; Columbia University Press, 2012.

———. "The Generation of Postmemory." In *On Writing with Photography*, edited by Karen Beckman and Liliane Weissberg, 202–30. Minneapolis: University of Minnesota Press, 2013.

Hochberg, Gil Z. *Becoming Palestine: Toward an Archival Imagination of the Future*. Durham: Duke University Press, 2021.

"Interview with Larissa Sansour." *Vector*, March 31, 2018. https://vector-bsfa.com/2018/03/31/interview-with-larissa-sansour/.

Jayyusi, Lena. "Iterability, Cumulativity, and Presence: The Relational Figures of Palestinian Memory." In *Nakba: Palestine, 1948, and the Claims of Memory*, edited by Ahmad H. Sa'di and Lila Abu-Lughod, 107–33. New York: Columbia University Press, 2007.

Jedlowski, Paolo. "Memory and Sociology: Themes and Issues." *Time and Society* 10, no. 1 (2001): 29–44.

Kaplan, E. Ann. *Climate Trauma: Foreseeing the Future in Dystopian Film and Fiction*. New Brunswick: Rutgers University Press, 2016.

———. "Visualizing Climate Trauma: The Cultural Work of Films Anticipating the Future." In *The Routledge Companion to Cinema and Gender*, edited by Kristin Lené Hole, Dijana Jelača, E. Ann Kaplan, and Patrice Petro, 407–16. London; New York: Routledge, 2017.

LeMaster, Lore/tta, and Amber Johnson. "Speculative Fiction, Criticality, and Futurity: A Critical Introduction." *Communication and Critical/Cultural Studies* 18, no. 3 (2021): 280–82.

Levy, Lital. "Temporalities of Israel/Palestine: Culture and Politics." *Critical Inquiry* 47 (Summer 2021): 675–98.

Lionis, Chrisoula. *Laughter in Occupied Palestine: Comedy and Identity in Art and Film*. New York: Bloomsbury, 2016.

Moore, Lindsey. "Suspended Between the Past and the Future: Larissa Sansour in Conversation with Lindsey Moore." In *Research/Practice 03: Larissa Sansour Heirloom*, edited by Anthony Downey, 110–30. London: Sternberg Press, 2019.

Muller, Nat. "Before and After a Disaster: Unsettling Representation in Larissa Sansour's 'Heirloom.'" In *Research/Practice 03: Larissa Sansour Heirloom*, edited by Anthony Downey, 6–22. London: Sternberg Press, 2019.

Nizar Zuabi, Amir. "The Underground Ghetto City of Gaza." *Haaretz*, August 4, 2014. www.haaretz.com/opinion/2014-08-04/ty-article/.premium/the-underground-ghetto-of-gaza/0000017f-e4dc-d9aa-afff-fddca82e0000?v=1678903419468.

Parikka, Jussi. "Middle East and other Futurisms: Imaginary Temporalities in Contemporary Art and Visual Culture." *Culture, Theory and Critique* 59, no. 1 (2018): 40–58.

Rosenfeld, Aaron S. *Character and Dystopia: The Last Men*. London; New York: Routledge, 2020.

Sa'di, Ahmad H., and Lila Abu-Lughod. "Introduction: The Claims of Memory." In *Nakba: Palestine, 1948, and the Claims of Memory*, edited by Ahmad H. Sa'di and Lila Abu-Lughod, 1–24. New York: Columbia University Press, 2007.

Said, Edward W. *The Question of Palestine*. New York: Vintage Books, 1979.

Sansour, Larissa. "Archeology in Absentia." *Larissa Sansour Website*. Accessed May 17, 2023. https://larissasansour.com/Archaeology-in-Absentia-2017.

Suleiman, Lama. "Afrofuturism and Arabfuturism: Reflections of a Present-day Diasporic Reader." *Tohu*, June 12, 2016. http://tohumagazine.com/article/afrofuturism-and-arabfuturism-reflections-present-day-diasporic-reader.

Weizman, Eyal. *Hollow Land: Israel's Architecture of Occupation*. London: Verso, 2007.

5 Decolonizing, Deterritorializing

Gaza and Beyond in the Films of Basma Alsharif

Decolonizing form, Depicting Gaza

Both *Home Movies Gaza* (2013) and *Ouroboros* (2017) are rooted in the Gaza strip, a landmass of around 343 km^2 that had a population of over 2 million when I began writing this book, before the genocide that began in October 2023.[1] When not the site of an active military siege, Gaza is a space of biopolitical warfare by other means: its borders are heavily controlled, mobility is extremely restricted and access to the most basic elements needed to sustain life is often withheld or intentionally disrupted. *Home Movies Gaza* is fully situated in the strip, while *Ouroboros* (Alsharif's first feature-length experimental work) is framed by sequences in Gaza but moves through three other countries and four other settings. *Ouroboros* explores the ways in which Gaza acts as a microcosm for other times and places, forging connections perhaps best framed as transnational, or as what Steven Salaita has termed "inter/nationalist."[2] Inter/nationalism is a decolonial thought and practice, mixing "solidarity, transnationalism, intersectionality, [and] kinship or intercommunalism" with a "commitment to mutual liberation based on the proposition that colonial power must be rendered diffuse across multiple hemispheres through reciprocal struggle."[3] In some ways, *Ouroboros* is a companion piece to the earlier *Home Movies*: beyond the Gaza connection, the films share formal strategies, if using them to different ends. The ouroboros is a symbol of a snake eating its tail, signifying the cycle of life, death and rebirth, and in the film, Gaza becomes a symbol of the potential for renewal, connecting many times, places and peoples. Via its temporal and spatial experiments, *Ouroboros* raises crucial questions about what is at stake in claims to national identity predicated on linear revolutionary narratives.

In these films, Alsharif develops an audiovisual and conceptual vocabulary to probe several aporetic dimensions of Palestinian identity. In invoking the aporia, I indicate a space of irresolvable lived contradiction that Kamran Rastegar suggests exists in part because the Palestinian situation remains unresolved and the violence ongoing.[4] Although he focuses on narrative and documentary film, Rastegar writes that "what remains most evocative

DOI: 10.4324/9781003474449-5

of the Palestinian story is its frequent irreconcilability to traditional narrative forms."[5] Alsharif's experimental practice addresses this irreconcilability in its independence from traditional narrative, its ability to shuffle easily between the documentary and the fictional and the ways in which it mobilizes elements of form to raise key questions around a situation that can feel increasingly hopeless. She explores alternative ways of delineating Palestinian visibility, through experimental visualities. The question of how to represent a population and situation that are so overdetermined in terms of their media representation, and at the same time so invisible (in that these representations lack dimension and deny Palestinians complex humanity), is explored in the work of the other filmmakers discussed in this book. Manna mines the historical archive for alternate narratives and figures through which to explore Palestine as an idea and a diverse demographic and offers portraits of decolonial resistance that center on struggles involving plants, waged by intelligent, funny and charming characters. Sansour leans into genre, exploring Palestinianness in fictionalized spaces and times. Bracketing victimhood allows her to foreground the impossibility of the current situation while also bringing out the universal dimensions of Palestinian experience. Alsharif's work innovates visually and acoustically to push back, at times in a Brechtian manner, on an audience so used to consuming images of Palestinian victimhood and suffering.

Spatially and temporally, Alsharif's films explore questions that have also been raised in the other films discussed here. The attempt to claim space that we saw in Sansour's *A Space Exodus* and *Nation Estate*, and the feeling of being without roots depicted in her untethered astronaut, become in Alsharif's *Home Movies Gaza* an exploration of extreme spatial containment, by contrast with the diasporic and expansive feelings generated by the strategies of *Ouroboros*. Gaza as a prison or reservation versus a cosmopolitan diaspora in search of a ground to claim are aporetic experiences of spatiality explored through Alsharif's decolonial formal vocabulary.

Finally, the issues of temporality and memory explored in the work of Manna and Sansour are singularly represented in Alsharif's work, particularly in her invocation of circularity and the eternal return in *Ouroboros*. We saw how Sansour moves out of trauma/*Nakba* time and draws on future anteriority to open up what Palestine will have been, and how Manna mines history to renarrate Palestine through fantasy echoes and forms of haunting. Alsharif's decolonial approach to temporality includes both the invocation of cyclical temporalities and also strategies of temporal reversal. In *Home Movies Gaza*, we feel the temporality of *sumud* as waiting; in *Ouroboros*, we move beyond *al-awda* (the return) as a teleological time to a time of repetition and reversal.[6] It is in *Ouroboros* that Gaza becomes a microcosm for (settler-)colonialism and racial violence as transnational and transhistorical phenomena. The film honors the struggles of Gazans through connection: it creates filmic links to other spaces and peoples and suggests that another world is possible.

Regarding Palestine: *Home Movies Gaza* (2013)

Home Movies Gaza interrogates the terms through which Gaza is accessed by an outside audience while still managing to offer an affective portrait of Gazan living conditions. It begins with a tracking shot of Gaza that runs around three and a half minutes. From the perspective of a moving vehicle, people of all ages, graffiti-covered walls, UN vehicles and uninhabited, unfinished buildings pass before the camera. We hear wind blowing, motors running, cars honking and human voices on the soundtrack. The footage is played in reverse, giving it a quality of strangeness whose source isn't immediately evident. The opening tracking shot briefly cuts and continues, passing a fenced beach, with the soundtrack resolving to the music of Abdelwahid Doukkali (*L'ehla yzid ktar*). The flattening effect of this tracking shot produces a walled-in feeling, revealing only a surface. Through this opening long take, the film introduces us to a Gaza, but one that does not allow itself to be fixed in our gaze through the camera's continual reversed movement.

The music heard on the beach bridges to a domestic setting, where a woman listens to Doukkali's song on her handheld radio before the transmission cuts to a news broadcast. On a black screen the words appear: "<MINISTER OF HEALTH, GAZA CITY: CONCERNING HEALTH CONDITIONS IN RELATION TO HUMAN RIGHTS.>" The woman reappears in a medium shot, seated and backlit, her face obscured. She begins to recite from *Lord of the Flies*, of a "time when hope was not necessary and therefore forgotten." These words, while spoken in Arabic, appear in white English text over her image (Figure 5.1). A long cross dissolve introduces men working along the Gazan shore, accompanied by the sounds of the sea. A male voice joins in the recitation of Golding's text. The words become doubled aurally and visually, reproduced in duplicate on the screen. As the sea takes precedence visually, the sound of drones emerges on the soundtrack, and droning remains an aural motif throughout *Home Movies*. Several sequences later, a young girl practicing the cello repeatedly bows a single note. Eventually the drone of the cello is replaced by a scale, while the sound of real drones (unmanned aerial vehicles (UAVs)) enters, along with an asynchronous dialogue between a mother and her son (also appearing as onscreen English text over the image of the young cellist). The mother has warned her son not to play outside and asks him if he is crazy. "Yes, I am crazy," he replies, as we hear what sounds like an explosion.

Alsharif uses the sound of drones to affectively and conceptually conjure the daily violence Gazans experience, without reproducing the spectacle of their suffering. In an early sequence, handheld cameras follow turkeys, horses, chickens and cats in a yard. These mundane scenes become infused with a potential violence through the use of visual effects. The animals appear blue in places, as if being seen through honing technology. A running time stamp further reinforces this impression on the images. The imagery suggests

Figure 5.1 The obscured figure in *Home Movies Gaza* (2013).

that the targeted destruction of the land and all its inhabitants is central to the Israeli occupation while also highlighting its dehumanizing effects. At one moment, a fly lies on its back atop a floral table cloth, unable to move (Figure 5.2). Digitally imposed blue markings distinguish the fly's body as the timer runs on the screen, suggesting its status as a sitting target. Struggling to right itself, the stagnation, immobility and surveilled condition of the fly produce a powerful visual metaphor for daily life in the Gaza Strip. The film suggests that even a cat or an insect register as a threat, when location is read only through the lens of risk.

Drones—as soundscapes and as technologies of visualization—are also central to *Ouroboros*. The film begins and ends in Gaza, with spectacular drone shots of the Gazan shore starting the film. Waves lap backwards, and cars run in reverse, echoing the reversal of footage in *Home Movies Gaza* and in her earlier film *O, Persecuted*, discussed in the book's introduction, where images of the filmmaker marking over the 1974 film *Our Small Houses* (Kassem Hawal) play in reverse. In *Ouroboros*, as the sunny aerial shot of the shore begins to spin, it dissolves over drone footage of destruction and debris from the aftermath of a bombing (Figure 5.3). The soundtrack abruptly changes from a droning hurdy-gurdy to the sound of flying drones. We briefly see a man from above, standing atop the rubble, giving a sense of the large-scale destruction—blocks of homes reduced to piles of stone. A seamless cut returning to the overhead track away from the beach offers audiovisual relief. It is relatively quiet except for a few honks; the buildings appear functional and bright in the sun. Gaza seems peaceful and livable. The editing and

Figure 5.2 A housefly as visual metaphor in *Home Movies Gaza* (2013).

Figure 5.3 Drone footage of Gaza in *Ouroboros* (2017).

cinematography here play with *Ouroboros'* interest in cycles of renewal and destruction, moving us through destruction and back again. The use of drone footage, reinforced by various forms of droning on the soundtrack, evokes the militarized reality of everyday life under settler colonialism and Israel's production of the Palestinian-as-target. As with the use of drone sounds and visual effects in *Home Movies Gaza*, these formal choices avoid explicit representations of violence while signifying ongoing suspended violence. By suspended violence, I refer to Ariella Azoulay and Adi Ophir's discussion of the containment of Palestinians through walls and checkpoints, constant surveillance, the ever-changing rules and regulations that determine their daily existence and the omnipresence of Israeli soldiers.[7] Suspended violence works in tandem with spectacular forms of violence, such as the raid or the bomb attack, and always contains the threat of the latter's sudden eruption, permeating daily life with stresses, anxieties, humiliations and shame. The immobilized and targeted housefly in *Home Movies Gaza* metaphorizes the everyday, non-newsworthy and omnipresent violence for Gazans. The use of drone footage in *Ouroboros* renders the visibility of Gaza inseparable from its production as a military target.

Alsharif again evokes militarized technologies of vision in her use of nighttime shooting in the final tracking shot of *Home Movies*, documenting the environs of a Gazan home. An extended POV shot travels through a yard (again, shown in reverse), the dominant green and black palette evoking night vision technology. Close-up patches of green foliage emerge from the blackness, while helicopters and other militarized sounds comprise the audio. The sequence conjures a situation of war and evokes colonial tropes of dark, savage continents. In this nighttime passage through the garden, Alsharif affectively registers the ongoing settler colonial violence. The anxiety effected by the soundtrack and the unsettling feeling of reversed footage, again infuse an otherwise quotidian space with a sense of threat, asking the viewer to consider what kind of Gaza comes into existence in its representation. The means of visualization here are the message, referring to the conditions of ongoing occupation, suspended violence and what Jasbir Puar calls the debilitation of the population in Gaza while avoiding the spectacularization of this condition.[8] The film's decolonial politics interrogate the terms by which Palestinians are seen through the colonial gaze.

Home Movies Gaza asks how the militarization of daily life renders impossible the very kinds of banal images that the home movie tradition takes for granted. Both the home movie tradition and the name Gaza evoke overdetermined representational conventions—but ones diametrically opposed. Significantly, the film does not offer either of the clichéd image sets suggested by the title, while Alsharif's persistent gaze on domestic spaces makes visible the impossibility of divorcing colonial occupation from the most intimate spaces of lived experience. This refusal to depict the suffering of Gazans is a critique of the Western media's documentation of the region that has predominated post-Oslo accords. The film replaces stereotypical images of suffering from the region, whose circulation has not produced any meaningful change in the daily life of Gazans, with a feeling of occupation that demands the spectator's reflection. The absence of humanized Palestinians in the larger global imaginary is foregrounded by the absence of figures in the film and the disturbance of their images when they do appear. *Home Movies* disrupts the consumption of even banal images of Palestinian life, insisting we read them through the everyday violence of occupation.

When Alsharif does engage tropes of victimization in her work, they are mediated and confrontational. For example, the final sequences of *We Began by Measuring Distance* (2009) include slowed-down footage of Palestinian women fleeing an attack. As one woman's distraught face occupies the screen, she asks, "For whom are you shooting us?" Here, the translation brings out a double meaning in "shoot." The journalist's camera is equated with the weapons of attack, as the victims ask whom these images are serving.[9]

Other Palestinian filmmakers have engaged the aporetic nature of visibility under the occupation. Oraib Toukan's *When Things Occur* (2016) consists entirely of Skype interviews with photojournalists who are also Gaza residents. The local photographers discuss their internationally circulated images, describing how different it is to photograph destroyed homes or families who have lost children, when you have undergone the same experiences. The ethics of documenting tragedy (and thereby advancing one's career) are foregrounded through confessions that gesture to the inherently exploitative nature of documenting others' pain. The complexities of what it means to document from inside rather than outside (nonetheless often for an outside audience) shape Toukan's film. Visually, the photographs are shown in desktop format, either as a series of copies of the same image in different resolutions, as might be seen in a Google image search, or as a single copy of the image, slowly zoomed in on to the point of abstraction. The repetition of the image within one frame and the enlarged pixelated close-up both problematize the referentiality of the image and, instead, foreground the issues surrounding the production and consumption of images of suffering. As Toukan theorizes:

> It is in the indecipherable, in the point of total abstraction of a figuration, where one can transcend representation altogether, *into* a sphere of political consciousness. And in turn, it is in *navigating* across the various planes of a micro, hyper-visual field at the level of the pixel-grain, in an almost haptic quality (when it *feels* like it can be touched and in turn becomes touching), where one can begin to fathom injustice.[10]

For Toukan, the representational image is a "cruel image," perpetuating the violence of war in its easy consumption by viewers. By navigating the image to the point of indiscernibility, we disrupt its ability to function as mere data (to be scrolled through among other images) or as a reproduction of colonialist imaginaries. Nor can it simply be assimilated as an image resembling the many others seen in other conflicts. By entering into the image and forgoing our visual mastery, Toukan suggests we start to *feel* (to be touched), and this is the beginning of a more ethical engagement, which recognizes how "co-optable the picture of suffering can be, and how it can seamlessly turn into an efficient instrument of fear by the perpetrator—into a one-for-all deterrent—like a cruel trophy of war."[11] At one point, Toukan's mouse cursor tenderly removes the pixelated blood off of the cheek of a young girl who survived a school bombing (Figure 5.4). The film probes the limits of witnessing and documenting while suggesting a desire to erase the compounded cruelty of the violent event and its photographic capture.

Relatedly, several films of Palestinian-Canadian artist Rehab Nazzal privilege a haptic experience of violence over visual representations of suffering. Nazzal's *Military Exercise in the Negev Prison* (2014) provides only audio and translated subtitles over a black screen. The audio comprises the terrifying and humiliating commands of IDF officers doing a "routine" training exercise with Palestinian political prisoners. The final titles inform that the exercise resulted in one death and 300 injured prisoners. The refusal to show, while being forced to listen, challenges the predominantly visual modes through which we are asked to bear witness to human rights violations. This mode of address is much less consumable than a still image, more visceral and demanding in our engagement and more horrifying because we cannot distance ourselves from or visually master the content.

Nazzal's earlier *A Night at Home* (2009) documents an Israeli night raid in the artist's hometown of Jenin in 2006. The screen is almost completely dark, with the sounds of voices, dogs barking and gunshots seemingly growing ever closer. The family discuss in hushed tones what is happening as they try to make sense of the sounds they are hearing and, implicitly, assess whether they or anyone close to them is in danger. The film thrusts us into the phenomenological experience of suspended violence, which is here premised precisely on its invisibility—people are taken away or murdered in the dark of night,

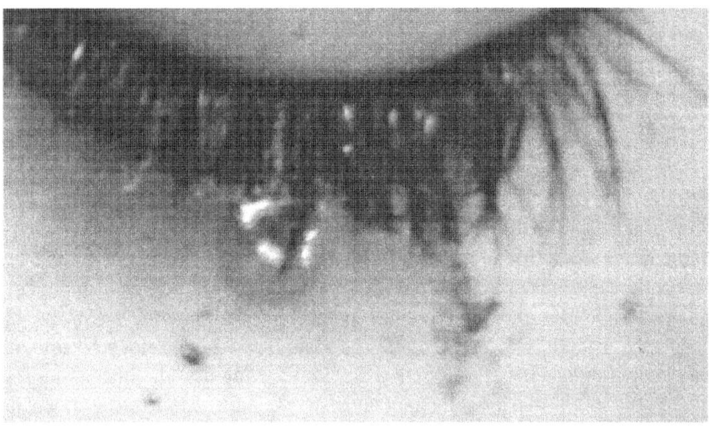

Figure 5.4 Still from Oraib Toukan, *When Things Occur* Single-channel video, 2016, color, sound, 28′. Courtesy of the filmmaker.

reminded as they lay in their beds of their subordinate and precarious position as occupied subjects. Both of these films by Nazzal force the spectator into a position of vulnerability. To watch is to listen, rather than to visually master, and to be open to the felt experience of a senseless and limitless violence.[12]

These artists, like Alsharif, explore how to ethically represent the experience of violence without sensationalizing it or objectifying its victims. *Home Movies* foregoes showing the suffering body altogether (acoustically or visually). When we do see bodies in the film, their appearance is mediated through disturbances in vision or sound. The body of the woman who recites from *Lord of the Flies* is backlit with English text placed prominently over her figure (see Figure 5.2). When we see the girl playing cello, a dissonance between image and referent is affected by the use of non-synch sound. The film's general absence of a focus on the human form is exemplified by a shot of a glitchy television set playing in an eerily empty living room (Figure 5.5). The same television set appears in *Ouroboros*, and its use in both films points to the spatial aporias explored in Alsharif's work.

Feeling the Space: *Ouroboros* (2017)

The first 20 minutes of *Ouroboros* take place in Gaza: Following the drone footage of the Gazan coast, a nine-minute sequence shot follows a caretaker through an unoccupied home.[13] By maintaining some level of activity in the house, the caretaker's labor is intended to deter the Israeli military

Figure 5.5 A glitchy nature program plays in an empty room in *Home Movies Gaza* (2013).

from misreading the empty home as a weapons cache.[14] In a circular tour, she guides us through each room and the surrounding yard as she tidies and rearranges its dormant contents. As mentioned, the home's living room also appears in *Home Movies Gaza*, in the scene where a television program plays to an empty room (see Figure 5.5). In *Ouroboros*, the television is off, and we see the slipcovers protecting the unused furniture (Figure 5.6). Shot with a steadycam, this long sequence shot plays in reverse, giving it an uncanny quality, reinforced by a soundtrack of Tibetan singing bowls. A dystopian ominous feeling predominates as circularity and reversal are reinforced as major themes within the film, already invoked in its earliest drone footage of the coast.

Pausing on the two films' depictions of the same living room highlights the contradictory Palestinian experiences of space explored. In *Home Movies Gaza*, the glitchy television program evokes the debilitation of informational infrastructures in the occupied territories (see Figure 5.5). As Omar Jabary Salamanca noted in 2001, Israel's control over the "one fiber optic cable, . . . that connects the entirety of Gaza to the outside world" reflects a "new colonial reality whereby infrastructural networks gain force as geopolitical sites to assert spatial control and as biopolitical tools to regulate and suppress life."[15] By contrast, *Ouroboros* is less focused on the containment or spacio-cidal conditions of the occupation and more concerned with connecting Gaza to other places and times.[16] After the home tour, the film switches to a series of moving shots with the same interior, focusing on details. English text appears

Figure 5.6 The same television in the tour of an unoccupied home in *Ouroboros* (2017).

onscreen, read in Chinook Wawa. The voiceover speaks of loss as we view the lifeless domestic objects:

> Refusing to disappear.
> As you recede our memories are replaced with emotions. . .
> As long as we don't move from where we are we can pretend to be elsewhere.
> And as long as we remain in this void, we can imagine we have not left.
> And have nothing left but to settle into a darkness.
> To get comfortable in our new homes.

Note that these themes echo those in Sansour's work, particularly the idea of the present as a void and the role of memory and emotion in maintaining identity. However, Alsharif moves on to do something entirely different with this Palestinian structure of feeling.

While all previous indications have suggested a film whose concerns are centered on Gaza and will remain with the Palestinians, it then leaves the occupied territory through an extended dissolve, slowly superimposing a new location in Los Angeles (LA) over Gaza. The long dissolve into a new space suggests we read these locations through and with one another. Soon, we enter a home in LA, and throughout the film, the Gazan home is rendered only one interior space among many in which we explore domestic actions. We watch our lead actor prepare food in an apartment in Matera, Italy, read for pleasure in a Chateau in France and observe others cooking in LA. These are perhaps iterations of the new homes that one has to "get comfortable in" per the voiceover. *Ouroboros* explores the other side of a Palestinian experience of space: rather than the confinement and spacio-cide of Gaza in *Home Movies*, the spatial impulse in *Ouroboros* is expansive, employing filmic techniques that evoke a sense of constant movement across spaces and times, attempting to connect the isolated and largely immobile Gazan population to the rest of the world through related global histories of colonization and war, but also of forgetting and renewal.

It is difficult to attribute a plot to *Ouroboros*: The film is almost dialogue-less.

A male character goes (in order) to LA, Matera, the Mojave and a 13th-century chateau in Brittany, bookended by scenes in Gaza. We watch him perform activities, such as building a greenhouse in the desert, playing ping pong and falling in and out of love with three different women, starting anew after each end.

The film uses structural principles to link the various spaces and activities: shots of objects are repeated (e.g., portraits or chandeliers unique to each location appear in different sequences), as are the movements of actors.[17] Sound bridges link geographical locations, and music recurs across spaces

Figure 5.7 A dissolve connects France and Gaza in *Ouroboros* (2017).

(Mendelssohn's *Songs Without Words*). Repeated tracking shots from cars and the use of extended crossfades contribute to the film's porous fluidity between spaces and times, resonating with the free-floating mobility of the drone footage in Gaza that starts the film (Figure 5.7). The sense of connection to a larger world and history are also evoked cinematically through the disruption of linear time effected by reversing footage of mundane actions like boiling eggs and walking outdoors.

This formal repetition between spaces and times accumulates in *Ouroboros* to create a sense of unbounded anywhere and any-time-ness. Quoting Carlo Levi writing of his exile in Matera, a narrator reads in Italian, "Perhaps out of vanity, it seemed to me inappropriate that the place where I was condemned to live should not appear shut in, but spread out and almost welcoming."[18] The film's structuring voiceover reinforces its cosmopolitan variety of locations with a plurality of languages: from Chinuk Wawa (spoken by fellow filmmaker Sky Hopinka) to Italian to English.

These articulations of space explore the paradox of the extreme containment of some Palestinians on one hand and the condemnation to diasporic exile for others.[19] As Helga Tawil-Souri summarizes, Palestine is, "on the one hand arbitrary, stultifying, deteriorating and paralyzing; on the other hand, cosmopolitan, pluralistic, capacious and sweeping."[20] Samera Esmeir sees this mixture of dispersal and containment as central to Israel's targeting of the Palestinian population, which

> maintains and reproduces itself through the fragmentation of Palestine and the Palestinian people into different population groups—those in exile, in

> Gaza, in the West Bank, in the Galilee and the Triangle, and so on. The proliferation of Palestinian populations has resulted in diffuse "solutions" to diverse populations—solutions that do not consider the possibility that the very production of discrete populations and separate solutions is the main achievement of Israeli colonial rule.[21]

Michel Khleifi established the visual presence of the land in Palestinian cinema.[22] Nurith Gertz and George Khleifi argue that his films such as *Wedding in Galilee* (1987) and *Tale of Three Jewels* (1994) "reconquer" Palestinian territory and "sketch a map of the entire Palestinian space that does not recognize Israeli borders and checkpoints and marks the separate, specific features of the landscape, weaving them into one harmonious whole."[23] This desire to reestablish a unity of space, to visually possess the land as it existed before the occupation, is shifted in Alsharif's work, particularly in *Ouroboros*. There, connection and futurity are generated through movement across borders, rather than tethered to a specific landmass. In the tour of the Gazan home, the use of reversal and a defamiliarizing soundtrack temper any emotional identification, distancing the viewer from the space and provoking reflection.

Contrary to a strong tradition in Palestinian visual culture, Alsharif characteristically avoids the ubiquitous checkpoint altogether in her work, a marker of the division and fragmentation of space/existence so prominent in the occupied territories. Gertz and Khleifi note that Palestinian cinema after the First Intifada is dominated by roadblocks.[24] One of the tensions characterizing Palestinian "roadblock" films is between the fragmentation of space caused by the imposition of checkpoints and borders and the desire to recreate a more harmonious unified territory.[25] Alsharif veers away from this spatial tendency as well. In contrast with films that seek "wholeness, including the lost wholeness of the past,"[26] Alsharif refuses the comfort of wholeness or of any unitary notion of national identity while insisting on the debilitating conditions of Gaza.[27] Futurity and repetition across difference replace fantasies of past wholeness, particularly through the depiction of space in *Ouroboros*.

The spaces visited in the film offer connections and contrasts with Gaza. Scenes filmed in a chateau and its surrounding gardens in Brittany evoke the wealth of empire through paneled rooms full of artifacts, portraits in gilded frames and ornate furniture. Matera was chosen as a location by Alsharif because it is where Pasolini shot *The Gospel According to St. Matthew* (1964). After scouting Palestine, Pasolini decided that it didn't look enough like the biblical Palestine he envisioned. Ironically, it was within Italy itself that he found a place that had not "developed" and kept its "primitive" character, so much so that it could stand in as biblical Palestine. Shooting in Matera also provides a link to Carlo Levi's *Christ Stopped at Ebola*, quoted in the film and written after his year spent there in exile for his opposition to the fascist government. Rather than pin down a specific meaning for Matera, the film seems more interested in its many resonances: Matera as the primitive-within-Empire, and, thus necessarily, Palestine as a space marked by time, film as a source of representation and mythologization and political exile are all brought into play through the use of Matera as a location.

The LA scenes are the most Brechtian of the film. As if he were a ghost, the protagonist watches as other actors engage one another—a central couple goes through various domestic scenarios, and, at one point, the living room hosts a crowded casting call. In these sequences, actors have been chosen for their appearance; they tend to be typecast and offered circumscribed roles—the Native American, the Chicana, the black man.[28] They improvise lines and scenes based on these stereotypes. A tall black actor sings the confederate minstrel tune "Dixie" while others look on woodenly. Bodies resonate with history but also refuse history as identity through the Brechtian staging. The familiar is invoked only to be made strange. Just as *Home Movies Gaza* interrogates the lenses through which Gaza is made visible, the actors' performances question the terms through which their bodies achieve legibility. In evoking histories of settler colonialism and slavery via their central casting of characters who visibly evoke ethnic and racialized types, the scenes in LA and the Mojave (in which some of the same actors appear) speak to histories that intersect with that of Palestine. The film thereby references the solidarities that have been forged historically between black Americans and Palestinians, and Indigenous North Americans and Palestinians. I return to this in what follows, considering these connections in terms of transnational alliances and the politics of inter/nationalism after exploring Alsharif's decolonial temporalities.

Gaza Returns, Deterritorialized

As the advent of modernity is bound up with the history of colonialism, colonial temporality aligns with the notion of history as progress: time is the forward march by which the rest of the globe is civilized and uplifted by its European superiors. At the same time, colonialism relegates the colonized to a space outside of history and development, where the unchanging nature of the colonized is contrasted with the colonizer's evolving culture. Settler colonialism, as a particular form of colonization, also functions by rendering the colonized not coeval with those who claim their territory, but it lacks the general goal of modernizing the colonized. It is not that the colonized need to be brought into history, as in non-settler forms of colonialism, but rather, in their relegation to ahistorical status they are rendered "irrelevant, illegitimate, marginal and anomalous."[29] Unlike other European settler colonial projects (i.e., North America), Zionism "as a form of Jewish nationalism is expressive of a prior identity and did not emerge through the experience of settlement, even as it was consolidated through it."[30] Rachel Busbridge argues that the Zionist right of return is "not so much a cyclical renewal of a glorious past as a matter of divine providence ordained by God."[31] Against this divinely ordained progression of settler time, Palestinians are rendered not only outside of history but also "incidental to place."[32]

As we have seen, Palestinian filmmakers explicitly challenge both the sense that Palestinians are somehow outside the present historical moment and that there is no future for Palestine. Sansour and Manna engage themes of history and/or memory to challenge teleological notions of time. By staging contemporary struggles around land use, Manna territorializes the present, refuting the lie that Palestinians are incidental to the land and revealing a relational understanding of the environment. This makes time integral to space, shaped by active social processes of negotiation and refusal. The critique of Israeli agricultural "development" in her work reflects John Collins observation that "With its 'time-oriented' narratives of 'development,' Western colonization has always clashed with indigenous ways of knowing that are built upon a holistic, relational notion of place."[33] Sansour deploys the future anterior in order to generate lines of flight out of a stagnant eternal present bound to past trauma and asks what it might mean to forget in order to move forward. Her work actively constructs Palestinian futures that make clear that Palestinian experience is neither marginal nor anomalous but relevant to a broad swathe of human experience. In this respect, Sansour's work is in deep sympathy with Alsharif's *Ouroboros*.

Echoing its titular symbol, *Ouroboros'* decolonial temporality looks to cyclical notions of time to challenge dominant settler colonial temporalities and fictions of modernity as progress. In her description of the film, Alsharif explicitly evokes the eternal return as a structuring principle. Nayrouz Abu Hatoum has argued that the

> Palestinian future . . . does not follow a linear progression towards a telos of a nation state, instead it is one that is imbricated with the present and the past resembling a structure of cyclical time. In other words, *a* future for Palestine and Palestinians is contingent on past and present collective worlding, and it is also contingent on the working of the imaginative.[34]

Abu Hatoum further describes this as "a cyclical form of temporality in which there are multiple points of beginnings."[35] This is an apt description of *Ouroboros*, whose plotless movement is a series of vignettes that do not suggest any one necessary starting point. The film's experiment with time offers a singular response to a question posed by Greg Burris: "Is there a way to conceive of return so that it points not to the past but to the future?"[36]

The cyclicality of *Ouroboros* is highlighted through a main structuring principle: Recited in Chinook Wawa, with English text appearing onscreen, the film opens with the words "Dawn," "Noon," "Dusk" and "Night" shown in succession. "Dawn" reappears before we see the first drone footage of Gaza. These times of day return as markers throughout the film, moving through

Night and then reversing back to Dusk, Noon and Dawn again, foregrounding cyclical time and temporal reversals over linear conceptions of history. The use of Chinook Wawa, "an indigenous language that was driven to extinction and then revived," reinforces themes of death and renewal, as well as gesturing to shared settler colonial histories.[37] That the speaker is Sky Hopinka, whose films focus on Indigenous North America/Turtle Island, creates a link between settler colonial histories that the film's imagery further cements. Alsharif has said:

> Going to Gaza and bearing witness to a situation that has only grown worse over time, it occurred to me that with a return to life (basic survival, how to secure food, shelter, and medicine), Gaza may actually be reaching towards a future in which the Gazans have learned to survive despite the failure of humanity or democracy or politicians or aid to rescue them from their crisis.[38]

Resonating with the themes of survival we have seen in Sansour's films, the return to a basic state then is paradoxically a foundation from which to move forward, itself part of a cycle of renewal. This concept of return is not a fantasy of restoring the pre-traumatic (i.e., pre-*Nakba*) past, however much Alsharif's play with reversal experiments with the affective power of undoing time.

In *Ouroboros*, the tracking shot in reverse seems to express a desire to move back in time to reverse history or to erase traumatic memory—to access a time when, as the text read in *Home Movies* from *Lord of the Flies* states, "hope was not necessary." *Ouroboros* also uses a colonial novel as an intertext: *Heart of Darkness* is quoted in the voiceover narration and appears within the diegesis. The lead character attempts (unsuccessfully) to romance a woman with card tricks, interrupting her reading of Conrad's novella. The protagonist's tricks fail, both as card tricks and as tools of seduction, disrupting the novella's flashback narrative with playful, resilient repetition.

Tropes of savagery or barbarism are rerouted throughout Alsharif's *oeuvre* to challenge their use in reproducing (settler)colonial imaginaries. As noted, the animals targeted by honing technology in *Home Movies* reference the dehumanization of the colonized subject, re-deploying it to critique the occupation's suspended violence.[39] In *A Fieldguide to the Ferns* (Alsharif, 2015), images of *Cannibal Holocaust* (Ruggero Deodato, 1980) are intercut with footage of an airstrike on a Gazan home in 2014. Parallels are drawn between the two sets of images: both figure the destruction of homes and situate the locus of savagery in the colonizer. In *Cannibal Holocaust* the cannibalism is a response to the European anthropologist-filmmakers' violence against the natives, including the burning of their occupied homes. This footage in *Fieldguide* is shown on a laptop sitting in a New Hampshire cabin. A figure circles the cabin; ominous POV shots of the surrounding ferns evoke night vision and colonial fantasies of untamed wilderness. This nighttime exploration of foliage echoes the final sequence of *Home Movies Gaza*, permeating the medium of vision itself with potential violence.[40] The barbaric treatment of Palestinians in the occupied territories is justified as containing the threat of (Palestinians') savage violence. Savagery preempts savagery.

Notably, *A Fieldguide to the Ferns* also uses reversed footage: the missile strike on Gaza plays backwards, experimenting with the power of visual reversal to undo the traumas of the past. In *Home Movies* it is harder to see the utopian dimensions of the tracking shots in reverse, as they form bookends to images of the surveillance and regulation of daily life in Palestine. There, reversal permeates the footage with a sense of the strange or uncanny, demanding a closer look from the spectator and thus a more discerning gaze on the images viewed. Combined with references to technologies of violence, the reversal's uncanny qualities augment the sense of danger permeating the audiovisual field. In *Ouroboros*, reversed footage, coupled as it is with the deterritorializing logic of the film more generally, evokes the more positive sense of an ability to forget, to undo and to will otherwise. This is a reversal of history, a moving out of trauma, not to restore a lost paradise, but to rejuvenate the present, making space for new narratives and modes of Palestinian-ness. The voiceover shares the hope, "That we will have eventually forgotten it all and will finally be saved." In sum, the meanings generated by reversed footage in Alsharif's films are multiple but always ask us to look differently at Palestine, be it as it is represented in the present through its constraint by a certain narrative of the past or how new futurities can be generated from seeing otherwise.

In addition to the times of day that appear on screen and the film's use of repetitions in form, its loose narrative also centers on cycles of forgetting and renewal. As noted, *Ouroboros* depicts a series of romances. In the Mojave, the protagonist attempts to connect with two different women, while in Brittany he finds blissful coexistence with a third love interest. In the Matera sequence, the protagonist is completely alone, as if in exile from love. He shaves his head, emphasizing the ascetic nature of this time of solitude, before loving again. Just as he repeats his failed card trick, the protagonist continues to "try again" in love, as the text onscreen admonishes. Alsharif notes the aporetic nature of forgetting in an interview about the film: forgetting the agony of heartbreak enables one to love again, renewing the possibility of suffering.[41] This echoes the dialogue in Sansour's *In Vitro* where Alia wonders if, "Perhaps a loss of memories is essential to starting over?" and Dunia worries that "Forgetting makes you vulnerable to mistakes you already made once." In *Ouroboros*, love models a relationship to time and history.

Ouroboros modifies the trope of circularity in Palestinian literature and cinema. Nadia Yaqub has argued that post-Oslo and post-second Intifada films use the motif of the circular journey differently than Palestinian literature of the 1960s, the former originating in a time of revolutionary optimism.[42] In these earlier texts, the past is returned to in the interest of future revolution, as a way of imagining a future to come. By contrast, circular journeys in contemporary narrative films explore "how to live in a present political context that characters cannot change, rather than as an ideal past to be recreated in the future."[43] This reckoning with the present in a non-revolutionary mode resonates with the work of Alsharif. Yet, *Ouroboros* takes the circular theme analyzed by Yaqub to another level both through the transnational connections it forges and also via its invocation of the eternal return. These suggest the possibility that the present can and will change: the lead character is blessed with forgetting; his history does not hold him back.[44] The cycle's reiterations contain the potential for something different to emerge.

As a thought experiment, the eternal return seems to carry several advantages. It is godless, since the only afterlife is the one that we are living now. It is therefore a concept profoundly invested in the present—not only must the past be shed, but the present must be affirmed and experienced, rather than deferred in the name of a teleological nationalism. Alsharif's use of drones and digital steadycams to film the Gaza sequences of *Ouroboros* (as opposed to 16 mm in the other locations) is meant to evoke "the perpetual present . . . there is almost no history, no future in those scenes, they're just in the moment that they're in which is how we access Gaza."[45] Yet through the film's connective transitions Gaza starts to reach outside that stagnant present and connect with other experiences of settler colonialism and oppression. It suggests that what Gazans are experiencing now is not exceptional but something that has occurred and continues to occur in different forms—from the ongoing colonization of indigenous Americans to the enslavement and segregation of Black Americans. The use of Chinook Wawa and the casting in the sequences set in LA and the Mojave explicitly invoke these histories. In his book *Inter/nationalism*, Steven Salaita notes the "long tradition among Palestinian scholars, artists, and politicians of naming the colonization of North America as both a precursor and a complement to Zionist settlement."[46] For Salaita, forging relationships across settler colonial regimes in Occupied Palestine and North America/Turtle Island is crucial to their future emancipation and throws into question the colonial temporality assigned to Indigenous peoples on Turtle Island: "Natives are not a defeated precursor to impending Palestinian dispossession but contemporaneous agents who directly inform the conditions of Palestine just as Palestinians directly inform the conditions of Indian Country."[47] Indigenous colonization is ongoing as is indigenous resistance. The documentary *Spaces of Exception* (Matt Peterson and Malek Rasamny, 2019) is an example of this inter/nationalist connection building, in its focus on Palestinian refugee camps and Native American Reservations. The film examines the creative forms of community renewal and resistance present within these potentially stagnant and demoralizing spaces, connected by settler colonial oppression and by inspiring resilience. The non-exceptional nature of Palestine is also argued by Collins:

> The reality is that Zionism is far more ordinary and far less exceptional than either of these groups [i.e., some of its supporters *and* some of its

> critics] would care to admit. As a settler colonial project, it is embedded in a set of deep structures that continue to be constitutive of the world today.[48]

Eric Ritskes adds that a decolonial politics "demands we work across race and indigeneity."[49] Alsharif's film does this via its formal choices, connecting the heavily bordered Gaza to the unbounded phenomenon of oppression.

A long history exists between black activism in the United States of America and the Palestinian cause. Palestinian activists have often explicitly linked their struggles to civil rights activism in the United States, such as the painting of George Floyd on the apartheid wall or the 2013 protest in Hebron discussed by Burris, in which marchers wore masks of black leaders, like Martin Luther King Jr., and held portraits of Rosa Parks and Frederick Douglass.[50] Protesters wore shirts that said, "I have a dream" as they marched through sections of the street where only Jews were allowed. Conversely, after the Rodney King verdict in 1992, black activists referred to the uprising as L.A.'s Intifada.[51] There are also deep roots connecting the struggles of black South Africans to those of the Palestinians: the PLO were ardent supporters of an end to the apartheid regime and Nelson Mandela famously hugged Yasser Arafat shortly after his release from prison in 1990. A statue of Mandela was given to Ramallah from the city of Johannesburg in 2016, and South Africans have consistently seen in Palestine a mirror of their own conditions under apartheid rule. There is some discussion amongst scholars, such as Salaita, of the politics of connecting black struggles for equality with those of the Palestinians, insofar as using terms like "apartheid" to discuss Palestine may water down or detract from the nature of the occupation as a form of settler colonialism with its specific forms of biopolitics. Ritskes, by contrast, argues for a "productive slippage between colonialism and settler colonialism" which "allows different forms of solidarity to be opened, and also allows the recognition of the anti-Black settler colonial nature of Israeli occupation and how Palestinian futurities breach these main forms of occupation and colonial violence in transformative ways."[52] *Ouroboros* performs this slippage, making connections across races and indigeneity, fostering multiple transnational links with the physically isolated strip. For Burris, "Black-Palestinian imaginaries should be considered radical precisely insofar as they escape the exclusive identitarianisms of the settler-colonialist projects they contest."[53] That *Ouroboros'* protagonist is not played by a Palestinian but by the Italian artist Diego Marcon also troubles any identitarian readings. The hollow and stylized use of performance in the film further refutes essentialized interpretations, as actors who are easily typecast according to race or ethnicity either awkwardly perform an expected behavior, such that any realist indexicality is foreclosed, or perform actions undetermined by anything outside their singularity as humans. The minoritized subject cannot be defined in the film, just as *Home Movies* denies the viewer a consumable depiction of a Gazan resident. Apropos her own nomadic biography, Alsharif says that she wants "to unpack the idea that being bound to history, to our pasts, somehow gets in the way of our agency."[54] Histories of racism, forced displacement and genocide are evoked in relation to Palestine, but the film moves beyond those parameters as well, expanding the temporal and geographical range of the film's cyclical exploration.

Cycling back to the eternal return, *Ouroboros* asks how Palestinians can move forward without *ressentiment*.[55] For Nietzsche, resentment is rooted in a refusal to forget or to will otherwise: "Powerless against what has been done, he is an angry spectator of all that is past. *The will cannot will backwards*."[56] And, "*That time does not run backwards*, that is his wrath [italics mine]."[57] Intervening through technology, Alsharif *can* make time run backward, expressing a will to move beyond an identity rooted in a past with a limited future. The voiceover in *Ouroboros* describes freedom as a letting go where, "we shall bask in the warmth and the glow of forgetting." For Nietzsche, "there could be no happiness, no cheerfulness, no hope, no pride, no *present* without forgetfulness."[58] For Palestinians living in the occupied territories, forgetting is a fraught injunction given that the violence and trauma are ongoing and hardly confined to the past. This is part of the aporetic nature of this temporal frame—what is the balance between memory and forgetting? How does one imagine the threshold that hasn't been crossed when their imagination is beholden to the past and the present feels stagnant? How can one forget what has not yet ended? How can the imagination be freed from its oppressors in conditions of occupation and genocide? *Ouroboros* works to reframe the present through a decolonial temporality rooted in transnational connection.

As noted in the introduction, Alsharif fits broadly into the category of Palestinian Post-Third-Worldist filmmakers, no longer invested in unitary revolutionary nationalisms at the expense of internal difference and struggles for equality.[59] Decoloniality must also be intersectional. Applying this to themes of iteration, reversal and circularity, what I am suggesting more broadly here is that the move away from linear temporalities—which bolster fictions of the heteromasculine revolutionary subject and a bounded homogenous nation-state—and toward a nonlinear decolonial time—which foregrounds difference, repetition and forgetting—has multiple implications for how Palestinian identity and statehood are conceived.

Alsharif's sense that "history and national identity are withholding forces" is why she has been referred to as a " 'Post-Palestinian' artist."[60] *Ouroboros* ends with a montage connecting the various spaces, activities and people we have seen throughout the film one final time. A pulsing electronic soundtrack links images that echo each other across distance/difference: sky beside sky, building next to building, intercut with the central figure dancing (Figure 5.8). His joyous dance brings to mind Zarathustra's admonishment: "You higher men, the worst about you is that all of you have not learned to dance as one must dance—dancing away over yourselves! What does it matter that you are failures? How much is still possible!"[61] In other words, try again.

Figure 5.8 The lead actor dances in the final moments of *Ouroboros* (2017).

Figure 5.9 The unfinished message of *Ouroboros* (2017).

Before the ecstatic montage that ends *Ouroboros*, we see a striking image of children in Gaza from a drone's eye view. They draw neon flowers with chalk on the pavement and begin to spell a word: H—E—L (Figure 5.9). This image of an action in mid-cycle suggests the circular temporality of the film, as well as the many aporias conjured by Alsharif's work. Are they spelling "Hell," describing the spatial restriction of the occupied territories? Or, is the word "Help," a plea for a visibility that might bring change rather than serve the occupation? More hopefully, the children may be spelling "Hello"—initiating a new beginning and inviting connection across distance.

I have tried to speak alongside the films throughout *Decolonial Imaginaries*, in dialogue with their counterrepresentations and the complexities of Palestinian experience they evoke. Alsharif, Manna and Sansour each make distinctive interventions in present discourses around Palestine, toward deessentializing Palestinianness through multiple strategies such as historical reimaginings, dystopian futurisms and experiments with form. Their art offers perspective, hope and space for contemplation, with the goal of justice for Palestine and Palestinians, terms in search of a decolonized referent.

Notes

1 An older version of this chapter was published as Kristin Lené Hole, "Visual, Spatial and Temporal Aporias in the Post-Palestinian Films of Basma Alsharif," *Middle East Journal of Culture and Communication* 16, no. 4 (November 2023): 386–413.
2 Steven Salaita, *Inter/Nationalism: Decolonizing Native America/Palestine* (Minneapolis: University of Minnesota Press, 2016).
3 Salaita, *Inter/Nationalism*, ix.
4 Kamran Rastegar, *Surviving Images: Cinema, War and Cultural Memory in the Middle East* (Oxford: Oxford University Press, 2015).
5 Rastegar, *Surviving Images*, 96.
6 On these two temporalities, see Lital Levy, "Temporalities of Israel/Palestine: Culture and Politics," *Critical Inquiry* 47 (Summer 2021): 678.
7 Ariella Azoulay and Adi Ophir, "The Monster's Tail," *Roulotte* 5 (2011): n.p., https://roulottemagazine.com/2011/04/the-monster%E2%80%99s-tail-ariella-azoulay-adi-ophir/.
8 Jasbir K. Puar, *The Right to Maim: Debility, Capacity, Disability* (Durham: Duke University Press, 2017).
9 For a discussion of this film, see Gil Z. Hochberg, *Visual Occupations: Violence and Visibility in a Conflict Zone* (Durham: Duke University Press, 2015).
10 Oraib Toukan, "Toward a More Navigable Field," *E-flux Journal* 101 (June 2019): n.p., www.e-flux.com/journal/101/272916/toward-a-more-navigable-field/.
11 Toukan, "Toward."
12 Helga Tawil-Souri's *Isochronism (24 hours in Jabaa)* (2004) is also notable in relation to the films discussed here, as it uses the sounds of nighttime violence (in the West Bank) as the rhythmic metronome for a montage that juxtaposes the results of the attack with scenes of Palestinian daily life.
13 This is Alsharif's grandmother's home. Andréa Picard, "Future's Past and Present Uncertainty: Basma Alsharif in Conversation with Andréa Picard," *Mousse* 59 (2017): 238.

14 Picard, "Future's," 238.
15 Omar Jabary Salamanca, "Uplug and Play: Manufacturing Collapse in Gaza," *Human Geography* 4, no. 1 (2001): 23.
16 On "spacio-cide," see Sari Hanafi, "Explaining Spacio-cide in the Palestinian Territory: Colonization, Separation, and State of Exception," *Current Sociology* 61, no. 2 (2013).
17 Alsharif discusses this approach in Justine Smith, "*Ouroboros* and the Cycle of Violence: An Interview with Basma Alsharif," *Senses of Cinema* 85 (December 2017), www.sensesofcinema.com/2017/feature-articles/basma-alsharif-interview/.
18 Carlo Levi, *Christ Stopped at Eboli* (New York: Farrar, Strauss, and Giroux, 1947), 7.
19 See Helga Tawil-Souri, "Cinema as the Space to Transgress Palestine's Territorial Trap," *Middle East Journal of Culture and Communication* 7 (2014), and Samera Esmeir, "Colonial Experiments in Gaza," *Jaddaliyah*, July 14, 2014, www.jadaliyya.com/Details/27434/Colonial-Experiments-in-Gaza.
20 Tawil-Souri, "Cinema," 174.
21 Esmeir, "Colonial Experiments," n.p.
22 Nuritz Gertz and George Khleifi, *Palestinian Cinema: Landscape, Trauma, Memory* (Bloomington: Indiana University Press, 2008), 70.
23 Gertz and Khleifi, *Palestinian Cinema*, 82–83.
24 For more on this, see also Drew Paul, *Israel/Palestine: Border Representations in Literature and Film* (Edinburgh: Edinburgh University Press, 2020).
25 Gertz and Khleifi, 82–83.
26 Gertz and Khleifi, 159.
27 An emphasis on the diversity within Palestinian society is present in Khleifi's work, if less so in films coming out of the period between and after the First and Second Intifadas. I should note that the use of space in Elia Suleiman's films also deserves separate consideration.
28 Smith, "*Ouroboros*," n.p.
29 Rachel Busbridge, "Messianic Time, Settler Colonial Technology and the Elision of Palestinian Presence in Jerusalem's Historic Basin," *Political Geography* 79 (2020): 2
30 Busbridge, "Messianic time," 3.
31 Busbridge, 3.
32 Busbridge, 2.
33 John Collins, *Global Palestine* (New York: Columbia University Press, 2011), 123.
34 Nayrouz Abu Hatoum, "Decolonizing [in the] Future: Scenes of Palestinian temporality," *Geografiska Annaler: Series B, Human Geography* 103, no. 4 (2021): 399.
35 Abu Hatoum, "Decolonizing," 409.
36 Greg Burris, *The Palestinian Idea: Film, Media, and the Radical Imagination* (Philadelphia: Temple University Press, 2019), 76.
37 Picard.
38 Picard, 234.

39 Thanks to an anonymous reviewer for encouraging me to think more about the use of animals in relation to these themes.
40 On the colonial fantasies that underpin Israel's occupation of Palestine, see Achille Mbembe, "Necropolitics," trans. Libby Meintjes, *Public Culture* 15, no. 1 (Winter 2003): 24.
41 Picard, 239.
42 Nadia Yaqub, "Utopia and Dystopia in Palestinian Circular Journeys from Ghassān Kanafānī to Contemporary Film," *Middle Eastern Literatures* 15, no. 3 (2012).
43 Yaqub, "Utopia," 312.
44 Alsharif explicitly invokes Nietzsche in describing the film: "An homage to the Gaza Strip. Based on the eternal return." Portfolio, private communication.
45 Smith, n.p.
46 136.
47 Collins, *Global Palestine*, 20.
48 Salaita, 154.
49 Eric Ritskes, "Beyond and Against White Settler Colonialism in Palestine: Fugitive Futurities in Amir Nizar Zuabi's 'The Underground Ghetto City of Gaza,'" *Cultural Studies Critical Methodologies* 17, no. 1 (2017): 79.
50 Burris, *Palestinian Idea*, 12. The book provides a long discussion of transnational activism/identification between Palestine and the American civil rights movement.
51 Collins, 127.
52 Ritskes, "Beyond and Against," 80.
53 Burris, 123.
54 Maria Palacios Cruz, "In Conversation: Maria Palacios Cruz interviews Basma Alsharif," in *Women Artists, Feminism and the Moving Image: Contexts and Practices*, ed. Lucy Reynolds (London: Bloomsbury Academic, 2019), 115.
55 In *Hanan Al-Cinema*, Laura U. Marks discusses Egyptian sociologist, Anouar Abdel Malek, who in the 1960s "posited the Nietzschean argument that Arabs were animated by a resentment that autonomy and political self-determination would heal." *Hanan Al-Cinema: Affections for the Moving Image* (Cambridge: MIT Press, 2015), 5.
56 Friedrich Nietzsche, *Thus Spoke Zarathustra*, trans. Walter Kaufman (New York: The Modern Library, 1995), 139.
57 Nietzsche, *Thus Spoke*, 139–40.
58 Friedrich Nietzsche, *On the Genealogy of Morals*, trans. Walter Kaufmann (New York: Random House, 1967), 57–58.
59 Ella Shohat, "Post-Third-Worldist Culture: Gender, Nation, and the Cinema," in *Transnational Cinema: The Film Reader*, ed. Elizabeth Ezra and Terry Rowden (London; New York: Routledge, 2006).
60 Daryl Meador, "A Cinematic Rejection of Gaza's Isolation," *Electronic Intifada*, July 20, 2017, https://electronicintifada.net/content/cinematic-rejection-gazas-isolation/21131 and Palacios Cruz, "In Conversation," 118.
61 Nietzsche, 295.

Bibliography

Abu Hatoum, Nayrouz. "Decolonizing [in the] Future: Scenes of Palestinian Temporality." *Geografiska Annaler: Series B, Human Geography* 103, no. 4 (2021): 397–412.

Azoulay, Ariella, and Adi Ophir. "The Monster's Tail." *Roulotte* 5 (2011): n.p. https://roulottemagazine.com/2011/04/the-monster%E2%80%99s-tail-ariella-azoulay-adi-ophir/.

Burris, Greg. *The Palestinian Idea: Film, Media, and the Radical Imagination*. Philadelphia: Temple University Press, 2019.

Busbridge, Rachel. "Messianic Time, Settler Colonial Technology and the Elision of Palestinian Presence in Jerusalem's Historic Basin." *Political Geography* 79 (2020): 1–9.

Collins, John. *Global Palestine*. New York: Columbia University Press, 2011.

Esmeir, Samera. "Colonial Experiments in Gaza." *Jaddaliyah*, July 14, 2014. www.jadaliyya.com/Details/27434/Colonial-Experiments-in-Gaza.

Gertz, Nuritz, and George Khleifi. *Palestinian Cinema: Landscape, Trauma, Memory*. Bloomington: Indiana University Press, 2008.

Hanafi, Sari. "Explaining Spacio-cide in the Palestinian Territory: Colonization, Separation, and State of Exception." *Current Sociology* 61, no. 2 (2013): 190–205.

Hochberg, Gil Z. *Visual Occupations: Violence and Visibility in a Conflict Zone*. Durham: Duke University Press, 2015.

Hole, Kristin Lené. "Visual, Spatial and Temporal Aporias in the Post-Palestinian Films of Basma Alsharif." *Middle East Journal of Culture and Communication* 16, no. 4 (November 2023): 386–413.

Jabary Salamanca, Omar. "Uplug and Play: Manufacturing Collapse in Gaza." *Human Geography* 4, no. 1 (2001): 22–37.

Levi, Carlo. *Christ Stopped at Eboli*. New York: Farrar, Strauss, and Giroux, 1947.

Levy, Lital. "Temporalities of Israel/Palestine: Culture and Politics." *Critical Inquiry* 47 (Summer 2021): 675–98.

Marks, Laura U. *Hanan Al-Cinema: Affections for the Moving Image*. Cambridge: MIT Press, 2015.

Mbembe, Achille. "Necropolitics." Translated by Libby Meintjes. *Public Culture* 15, no. 1 (Winter 2003): 11–40.

Meador, Daryl. "A Cinematic Rejection of Gaza's Isolation." *Electronic Intifada*, July 20, 2017. https://electronicintifada.net/content/cinematic-rejection-gazas-isolation/21131.

Nietzsche, Friedrich. *On the Genealogy of Morals*. Translated by Walter Kaufmann. New York: Random House, 1967.

———. *Thus Spoke Zarathustra*. Translated by Walter Kaufman. New York: The Modern Library, 1995.

Palacios Cruz, Maria. "In Conversation: Maria Palacios Cruz interviews Basma Alsharif." In *Women Artists, Feminism and the Moving Image: Contexts and Practices*, edited by Lucy Reynolds, 115–26. London: Bloomsbury Academic, 2019.

Paul, Drew. *Israel/Palestine: Border Representations in Literature and Film*. Edinburgh: Edinburgh University Press, 2020.

Picard, Andrea. "Futures's Past and Present Uncertainty: Basma Alsharif in Conversation with Andréa Picard." *Mousse* 59 (2017): 232–39.

Puar, Jasbir K. *The Right to Maim: Debility, Capacity, Disability*. Durham: Duke University Press, 2017.

Rastegar, Kamran. *Surviving Images: Cinema, War and Cultural Memory in the Middle East*. Oxford: Oxford University Press, 2015.

Ritskes, Eric. "Beyond and Against White Settler Colonialism in Palestine: Fugitive Futurities in Amir Nizar Zuabi's 'The Underground Ghetto City of Gaza.'" *Cultural Studies Critical Methodologies* 17, no. 1 (2017): 78–86.

Salaita, Steven. *Inter/Nationalism: Decolonizing Native America and Palestine*. Minneapolis: University of Minnesota Press, 2016.

Shohat, Ella. "Post-Third-Worldist Culture: Gender, Nation, and the Cinema." In *Transnational Cinema: The Film Reader*, edited by Elizabeth Ezra and Terry Rowden, 39–56. London; New York: Routledge, 2006.

Smith, Justine. "*Ouroboros* and the Cycle of Violence: An Interview with Basma Alsharif." In *Senses of Cinema*, 85, December, 2017. www.sensesofcinema.com/2017/feature-articles/basma-alsharif-interview/.

Tawil-Souri, Helga. "Cinema as the Space to Transgress Palestine's Territorial Trap." *Middle East Journal of Culture and Communication* 7 (2014): 169–89.

Toukan, Oraib. "Toward a More Navigable Field." *E-flux Journal* 101 (June 2019): n.p. www.e-flux.com/journal/101/272916/toward-a-more-navigable-field/.

Yaqub, Nadia. "Utopia and Dystopia in Palestinian Circular Journeys from Ghassān Kanafānī to Contemporary Film." *Middle Eastern Literatures* 15, no. 3 (2012): 305–18.

Index

For Product Safety Concerns and Information please contact our EU representative GPSR@taylorandfrancis.com
Taylor & Francis Verlag GmbH, Kaufingerstraße 24, 80331 München, Germany

www.ingramcontent.com/pod-product-compliance
Lightning Source LLC
LaVergne TN
LVHW010930110826
845149LV00013B/2533

* 9 7 8 1 0 3 2 7 5 5 4 0 3 *